W9-AMN-857

799.08 McManus, Patrick F.
MC
A fine and pleasant
misery

© THE BAKER & TAYLOR CO.

A Fine and

Pleasant Misery

Also by Patrick F. McManus

They Shoot Canoes, Don't They?

A FINE AND PLEASANT MISERY

Patrick F. McManus

Edited and with an Introduction by
JACK SAMSON

Holt, Rinehart and Winston
New York

Published simultaneously in Canada by Holt, Rinehart
and Winston of Canada, Limited.

Library of Congress Cataloging in Publication Data

McManus, Patrick F
A fine and pleasant misery.

A selection of stories which originally appeared in
Field & Stream.
1. Fishing—Anecdotes, facetiae, satire, etc.
2. Hunting—Anecdotes, facetiae, satire, etc.
3. Camping—Anecdotes, facetiae, satire, etc. I. Title.
SH4441.M365   799'.08   77-13452
ISBN: 0-03-022811-5 Hardbound
ISBN: 0-03-059172-4 Paperback

All stories in this book originally appeared in *Field & Stream.*
The title story, "A Fine and Pleasant Misery," was first published
as "The Misery Kit."

Designer: Joy Chu

Printed in the United States of America

9 10 8

ISBN 0-03-022811-5 HARDBOUND
ISBN 0-03-059172-4 PAPERBACK

To Darlene and Mom

CONTENTS

Acknowledgments

I WOULD LIKE to acknowledge my debt to Jack Samson, editor of *Field & Stream,* who is largely responsible for bringing this book into existence; to Clare Conley, former editor of *Field & Stream,* who first detected some faint promise in me as a writer and whose encouragement and direction sustained me in the early years; to my mother, as an inexpendable source of wit and good humor; to my sister (The Troll) for provoking me into writing; to my wife, who corrects my spelling, grammar and taste; to my friend and colleague Dick Hoover, who daily endures the indignities of close association with a humorist; and to my friends Lloyd Humphrey and Vern Schultz, who have lived many of these stories.

Introduction

I GUESS Pat McManus sort of sneaked up on me. I had been editing his stories for a couple of years—from back around 1970—and I really didn't *read* Pat that much. Sometimes an editor is too busy editing to settle down and really enjoy the material.

Oh, I knew he was good and everyone on the staff kept telling me how funny he was. And there was the constant flow of reader mail demanding more of McManus in *Field & Stream.* A typical reader letter would go something like: "My husband and son have been subscribing to your magazine for years because they are both ardent hunters and fishermen, but I never read it because I am a golfer. But the other day I happened to read a story in *Field & Stream* by Patrick McManus. He is really funny! I think he is a riot! Now when the magazine comes in I look for McManus before I give the magazine to my husband or son. More! [Signed] Mrs. . . ."

Then one day one of Pat's stories came in and

I was not bogged down in some administrative chore; I put my feet up on the desk and began to read. The story was called "A Dog for All Seasons," and by the time I had gotten to the third page I was, literally, doubled over. My secretary said she had never—in all those years—heard me laugh so hard—or for so long. The more I read the funnier McManus became.

The damned dog, which he had as a kid and which you will read about in this collection of his best stories, was called Strange. His name in the beginning had been Stranger, wrote McManus, in the faint hope that he was just passing through when they first saw him. Strange was that most wonderful of all dogs: a mutt. A mutt with no redeeming features.

According to Pat, the dog had only two chores around his house: to attack prowlers, especially those whose character bore the slightest resemblance to his own, and to protect the chickens. On the second point, Strange always thought it was the other way around. He was also constantly making snide remarks about Pat's grandmother's cooking.

He insisted on following McManus when he went hunting or fishing—something Pat claims he tried to prevent.

"An army of Cossacks could have bivouacked on our front lawn for the night without his knowing a thing about it," McManus wrote, "but he could hear the sound of a shotgun shell being dropped into a flannel shirt pocket at a hundred yards."

Strange made slightly less noise going through the woods than an armored division through a bamboo jungle. Nevertheless, says Pat, they usually managed to get a few birds, apparently because the birds thought that anything that made that much noise couldn't possibly be hunting!

"My dog," says McManus of Strange, "believed

in a mixed bag: grouse, ducks, pheasants, rabbits, squirrels, chipmunks, gophers, skunks and porcupines. If we
saw a cow or a horse, he would shout 'There's a big
one! Shoot! Shoot!' "

Well, by now I am sure you see what I mean
about McManus and his sneaking up on you. I quickly
did three things: wiped the tears from my eyes; called
Pat at his home in Spokane, Washington; and offered
him a full-time job as an associate editor of *Field &
Stream*. I have never been sorry, and I am delighted the
editors of my competing outdoor magazines were just
enough dumber than I was about how funny Pat is. No,
I did four things, come to think of it. I dug up all the
back issues I could find in the office for which Pat had
written and took them all home with me that night. I
read every one of them, and my wife was so annoyed at
me for completely ignoring her that she went to have
dinner with her sister. I never knew she was gone until
she returned home at about midnight to find me sleeping on the den couch—a delighted smile still on my
face.

A number of you reading this will remember
the great American humorist Robert Benchley. You
younger readers may not, but you sure missed a funny
man if you never read anything he wrote. He used to
write for all sorts of magazines, especially the *New
Yorker*. He also wrote books, and I guess a lot of his
talent was inherited by his kids because a couple of
them also write—including his son Peter who wrote
Jaws.

Well, Pat McManus is the Bob Benchley of the
outdoors. When I heard my close friend and associate
Ed Zern say he thought Pat was one of the funniest
writers he had ever read I knew we had a winner,
because Ed—of "Exit Laughing" fame in *Field & Stream*
—has got to be one of the deans of outdoor humor.

We all have our favorite McManus stories and I guess mine (along with "A Dog for All Seasons") is "The Modified Stationary Panic"—also found in this collection which I have had the pleasure and privilege of editing. Pat was off on his own cloud nine about how easy it is to get lost in the woods and how the experts on survival caution everyone not to panic. Pat disagrees with this theory. He feels if one gets lost he or she should, especially if they are a panicker as is Pat, get the panic out of the system all at once. He claims that holding panic in may cause severe psychological disorders and even stomach cramps and baldness. Over the years, Pat says, he has been involved in several dozen panics, usually as a participant, sometimes simply as an observer.

"Most of my panics have been of a solitary nature," he says, "but on several occasions I have organized and led group panics, one of which involved twenty-some people. In that instance, a utility company took advantage of the swath we cut through the forest and built a power line along it."

Pat says back in the earlier days of his panicking he utilized what he refers to as the Full Bore Linear Panic (FBLP). This is where you run flat out in a straight line until the course of your panic is deflected by a large rock or tree, after which you get up and sprint off in the new direction.

"One time when we were kids," says Pat, "my friend Retch and I panicked right through a logging crew and the loggers dropped what they were doing and ran along with us under the impression we were being pursued by something. When they found out all we were doing was panicking, they fell back, cursing, and returned to their work."

Nowadays, Pat says, he will advise against undertaking a Full Bore Linear Panic unless, of course, one is equipped with a stout heart, a three-day supply of food, and a valid passport.

Only McManus could have thought up "The Great Cow Plot"—also contained in this collection. All of us have been harassed by cows while fly fishing for trout, but nobody but Pat could have realized the cows had gotten together and planned the war against us. Biologists and science-fiction buffs have speculated about the earth's takeover by the insect world, but Pat suggests perhaps the bovine species poses a far greater threat. Even when he plans a fishing trip forty miles back into the wilderness, he says, a herd of cows usually will get wind of it and go on a forced march to get there before Pat does.

"If I was on the nineteenth floor of a department store and stopped to net a guppy out of an aquarium," he says, "a cow would get off the elevator and rush over to offer advice."

Beginning to see what I am talking about? McManus is not only funny, there are more than a few suspicions around the *Field & Stream* editorial offices that just maybe Pat ain't wrapped all that tight! But if he *has* come unglued let us all hope he stays that way!

There is altogether too little humor in the outdoor field. What with all the protectionists telling us we are responsible for every endangered species from the Arizona pupfish to the California condor, we could use a few laughs—those of us who love the outdoors.

Like a great many fine writers Pat went into newspaper work upon graduation from Washington State University in 1956. Also, he has been a television reporter and later an English teacher. He earned an M.A. in English from his alma mater in 1962 and now teaches at Eastern Washington University—with the rank of professor.

But it is early life that prepared him for his

outdoor writing. He was born and raised in Idaho where his mother was a schoolteacher. He grew up on a small farm with a creek running through it—like the creek running through so many of his stories. He writes about the outdoors well because he has done a number of things in it besides fish, camp and hunt. He has been in heavy construction work, a truck driver, high scaler, grease monkey, and a groundman for a power line construction crew.

You will never forget his cast of characters—from his boyhood pal Retch; his mentor, old Rancid Crabtree; Grogan, of war surplus fame; Grandma; and least of all Strange, the dog with no redeeming features.

Look out world. Here comes Pat McManus!

Jack Samson, Editor
Field & Stream

A Fine and
Pleasant Misery

A Fine and Pleasant Misery

MODERN TECHNOLOGY has taken most of the misery out of the outdoors. Camping is now aluminum-covered, propane-heated, foam-padded, air-conditioned, bug-proofed, flip-topped, disposable, and transistorized. Hardship on a modern camping trip is blowing a fuse on your electric underwear, or having the battery peter out on your Porta-Shaver. A major catastrophe is spending your last coin on a recorded Nature Talk and then discovering the camp Comfort & Sanitation Center (featuring forest green tile floors and hot showers) has pay toilets.

There are many people around nowadays who seem to appreciate the fact that a family can go on an outing without being out. But I am not one of them. Personally, I miss the old-fashioned misery of old-fashioned camping.

Young people just now starting out in camping

probably have no idea that it wasn't but a couple of decades ago that people went camping expecting to be miserable. Half the fun of camping in those days was looking forward to getting back home. When you did get back home you prolonged the enjoyment of your trip by telling all your friends how miserable you had been. The more you talked about the miseries of life in the woods, the more you wanted to get back out there and start suffering again. Camping was a fine and pleasant misery.

A source of much misery in old-fashioned camping was the campfire, a primitive contrivance since replaced by gas stoves and propane heaters. It is a well-known fact that your run-of-the-mill imbecile can casually flick a soggy cigar butt out of a car window and burn down half a national forest. The campfire, on the other hand, was a perverse thing that you could never get started when you needed it most. If you had just fallen in an icy stream or were hopping around barefooted on frosted ground (uncommon now but routine then), you could not ignite the average campfire with a bushel of dry tinder and a blowtorch.

The campfire was of two basic kinds: the Smudge and the Inferno. The Smudge was what you used when you were desperately in need of heat. By hovering over the Smudge the camper could usually manage to thaw the ice from his hands before being kippered to death. Even if the Smudge did burst into a decent blaze, there was no such thing as warming up gradually. One moment the ice on your pants would show slight signs of melting and the next the hair on your legs was going up in smoke. Many's the time I've seen a blue and shivering man hunched over a crackling blaze suddenly eject from his boots and pants with a loud yell and go bounding about in the snow, the front half of him the color of boiled lobster, the back half still blue.

The Inferno was what you always used for cooking. Experts on camp cooking claimed you were supposed to cook over something called "a bed of glowing coals." But what everyone cooked over was the Inferno. The "bed of glowing coals" was a fiction concocted by experts on camp cooking. Nevertheless the camp cook was frequently pictured, by artists who should have known better, as a tranquil man hunkered down by a bed of glowing coals, turning plump trout in the frying pan with the blade of his hunting knife. In reality the camp cook was a wildly distraught individual who charged through waves of heat and speared savagely with a long sharp stick at a burning hunk of meat he had tossed on the grill from a distance of twenty feet.

The rollicking old fireside songs originated in the efforts of other campers to drown out the language of the cook and prevent it from reaching the ears of little children. Meat roasted over a campfire was either raw or extra well done, but the cook usually came out medium rare.

The smoke from the campfire always blew directly in the eyes of the campers, regardless of wind direction. No one minded much, since it prevented you from seeing what you were eating. If a bite of food showed no signs of struggle, you considered this a reasonable indication that it came from the cook pot and was not something just passing through.

Aluminum foil was not used much in those days, and potatoes were simply thrown naked into the glowing coals, which were assumed to lie somewhere at the base of the Inferno. After about an hour the spuds were raked out with a long stick. Most of the potatoes would be black and hard as rocks, and some

of them would be rocks, but it didn't make much dif-
ference either way. Successive layers of charcoal would
be cracked off until a white core of potato was uncov-
ered, usually the size of a walnut or maybe a pea. This
would be raw. Sometimes there would be no white core
at all, and these potatoes were said to be "cooked
through." Either that or they were rocks.

There were other fine sources of camping misery besides campfires. One of the finest was the old-
fashioned bedroll. No matter how well you tucked in
the edges of the bedroll it always managed to spring a
leak in the middle of the night. A wide assortment of
crawly creatures, driven by a blast of cold air, would
stream in through the leak. Efforts to close the gap
merely opened new leaks, and finally you just gave up
and lay there, passing the time until sunrise—approximately thirty-seven hours—by counting off insects one
by one as they froze to death on your quivering flesh.

My bedroll, made from one of my grandmoth-
er's patchwork quilts, was an oven compared to the first
"sleeping bag" I ever spent a night in. My inconstant
boyhood companion, "Stupe" Jones, told me one
September day that I would not need my bedroll on
our outing that night because he had discovered an
honest-to-goodness sleeping bag in the attic of his house
and it was big enough for both of us to sleep in. Now
when I saw what a compact little package a real sleeping
bag could be folded up into, I became immediately
ashamed of my own cumbersome bedroll, which rolled
up into a bundle the size of a bale of hay. I was glad
that I had not marred the esthetics of our little camping
trip by toting the gross thing along. That night we
spread the sleeping bag out on a sandy beach alongside
Sand Creek, stripped to our shorts (we had both been
taught never to sleep with our clothes on), and hopped
into the bag. The effect was much like plunging

through thin ice into a lake. Not wishing to insult my friend or his sleeping bag, I stifled a shrill outcry with a long, deep gasp disguised in turn as a yawn. Stupe said through chattering teeth that the sleeping bag was bound to warm up, since it was, after all, a sleeping bag, wasn't it? No two lovers ever clung to each other with such tenacity as did those two eight-year-old boys through that interminable night. Later we discovered that some sleeping bags come in two parts, one a nice padded liner and the other a thin canvas cover. What we had was the latter.

One of the finest misery-producing camping trips I've ever been on occurred when I was about fourteen. Three friends and I were hiking to a lake high up in the Idaho Rockies. What had been a poor, struggling drizzle when we left home worked its way up and became a highly successful blizzard in the mountains. Before long our climbing boots (called "tennis shoes" in more prosperous parts of the world) were caked with ice. The trail was slowly being erased before our very eyes, and I was beginning to write news stories in my head: "The futile search for four young campers lost in a snowstorm has been called off. . . ." As we clawed our way up the side of the mountain, one of the frailer souls—never ask me who—suggested that the better part of valor or even of stark madness might be to turn back. But he was shouted down with such cries as, "When I come this far to fish, I am going to fish!" and "Who knows which way is *back*?"

Eventually we came to the tiny cabin of a trapper, who had either been a midget or had crawled around on his knees all day, for the structure was only four feet from dirt floor to log ceiling. We tidied the place up by evicting a dead porcupine, split up enough wood to last a month, and started a fire in a little makeshift stove. The stovepipe was a foot short of the roof and this resulted in the minor inconvenience of having the roof catch fire every once in a while, but nobody really minded.

On the second day Kenny and I fought our way up to the lake, where he carried out his vow to fish, and then we stumbled back to the cabin. We stripped off our sopping clothes and sat down side by side on the woodpile next to the stove, whose glowing pipe was sending out soothing waves of heat from the flames howling up through it. Now as was our practice in those days, we had carried enough grub with us to feed a regiment of lumberjacks for a week of full-time eating, and Norm, a rather plump kid, decided to take the edge off his boredom by shooting "baskets" with an excess of hardboiled eggs he had discovered. The opening at the top of the stovepipe served as the "basket." Kenny and I watched in fascinated horror, as they say, as one of the rim shots lodged on the edge of the glowing pipe and the whole contraption began to topple toward our naked laps. Now both of us worked up a sizable amount of activity, but because of the cramped quarters, it was insufficient to move us clear of the descending pipe. In order to avoid incurrence of potentially worse damage to our anatomies we caught the stove pipe in our hands. For two or three hundredths of a second we passed the glowing cylinder back and forth between us, all the while calmly contemplating the best course of action, since neither one of us could manage to accumulate enough free time or leverage to get up from the woodpile. At last it occurred to us to simply drop the pipe on the floor, both of us wondering why we hadn't thought of such an obvious solution sooner. At the time it seemed that we had juggled the stovepipe for approximately two hours, but in retrospect, I doubt that the total time was more than half a second.

Smoke, true to its nature, had in the meantime filled the cabin to overflowing and the four of us rolled out through the tiny door hole as a single choking ball of adolescent humanity. The storm outside, particularly to those not wearing any clothes, was refreshing and seemed to call for some strenuous exercise. What followed, as Vern remarked later, was something you don't see every day: two naked and enraged people chasing an hysterical fat kid up the side of a mountain in the middle of a blizzard.

In terms of misery, that camping trip was very fine.

I once launched my family on a program designed to toughen them up, on the assumption that the more misery they could endure the more they would enjoy hunting, fishing, and camping. Whenever anyone skinned a knee or thumped his "crazy bone," he was to reply in answer to inquiries about the extent of his pain: "A mere detail." Thus my children were expected to ignore the minor miseries encountered in the acquisition of outdoor knowledge and experience, and to make little of mosquito bites, burned fingers, and that vast assortment of natural projectiles known as "stickers."

As it turned out, though, I had to abandon the program. One day on a family camping trip, I picked up a large branch for firewood and discovered an outlaw band of yellow jackets waiting in ambush. A running battle ensued. I finally outdistanced the little devils, as I called them, but not before several of them had inflicted some terrible wounds on various parts of my person. My family watched as I flitted like a nymph through the woods, careening off of boulders and leaping mammoth moss-covered logs. Fortunately, as my wife said later, most of my shouts were inaudible and the children were saved from traumas that might have wrought psychological havoc. When I finally lunged back into camp, still sweating and snarling, my littlest girl consoled me with the words, "Details, Daddy, mere details."

Well I decided right then and there if a kid can't distinguish between *real* pain and a little old skinned knee, then I had better call off the whole program, and that is what I did. I mean you don't want your children to grow up to be totally insensitive.

But camping misery is a thing of the past. Like most of my fellow outdoorsmen, having gathered unto the camper the fruits of technology, I am protected from cold by propane, from hardness by foam rubber, and from the insect world by a bug bomb. Still, sometimes I have a nostalgic yearning for some of that old-fashioned misery, and it came to me that what we need nowadays is a misery kit. I think it would find a market, especially among older campers, who might enjoy a bit of instant misery on a camping trip so they would have something to tell the folks back home about. There could be an aerosol can for spraying a blast of cold air down your back every once in a while, another for spraying smoke in your eyes. There might even be a pair of refrigerated boots that you could stick your feet into for a few minutes each morning. A rock or a pine cone could be included for slipping under the fitted sheet of a camper bunk. Everyone, of course, would want a pre-charred spud. There might even be a box of mixed insects—yellow jackets, mosquitoes, ticks, jiggers, and deer flies—but maybe that would be carrying misery a bit far.

A Dog for
All Seasons

ONE OF THESE DAYS they'll probably come out with a mechanical bird dog that locates pheasants with a special scent detector and radar. A small on-dog computer will record and analyze all available information and give the hunter a report: two roosters and five hens in stubble field—253 feet. A pointer on the dog's back would indicate the exact direction.

There would be luxury models, of course, with built-in stereo and FM sets, a special compartment for lunches, a cooler for beverages. The dog's nose would be a cigarette lighter.

The really high-priced jobs would not only retrieve the bird but pluck it, dress it, wrap it in foil, and quick-freeze it. By the time the bird got back to the hunter it would be neat and trim as a TV dinner.

Since no self-respecting hunter would want to be seen carrying his dog around by a handle, all but the cheapest models would be designed to look like nifty attaché cases. If you passed by some good hunting ground on your way home from work, you could get out and let your attaché case nose around in a thicket or two.

There would be minor inconveniences ("We'll have to go back, Harry. I thought I had my bird dog but it's just a bag of briefs."), but on the whole, the mechanical bird dog would have many advantages over the standard makes most of us have now.

Still, I'm something of a traditionalist, and if the mechanical bird dog were to go on the market tomorrow I'd probably stick with my old ready-made hound, such as he is. His eyes don't light up much anymore, let alone his tubes, and you can't light a cigarette on the end of his nose. The sounds that come out of him are not stereo (fortunately) and he has never been much on fidelity any way you look at it. But I would keep him nevertheless. There was a time in my youth, however, when I would have swapped my dog for a mechanical job and thrown in my T-shirt decorated with bottle caps to boot.

Take the flaws of character you find in all dogs and most human beings, roll them up in the hide of a sickly wart hog, and you would have a reasonable facsimile of my dog Stranger, who was dirty, lazy, bigoted, opinionated, gluttonous, conceited, ill-tempered, and an incorrigible liar.

An old man once summed up Stranger's character succinctly. "He's a prevert!" he said. I didn't know what preverts were but had no doubt Stranger was one of them.

We had called the dog Stranger out of the faint hope he was just passing through. As it turned out, the name was most inappropriate since he stayed on for nearly a score of years, all the while biting the hands that fed him and making snide remarks about my grandmother's cooking. Eventually the name was abbreviated to "Strange," which was shorter and much more descriptive.

My mother used to say that Strange was like one of the family. Then my grandmother would bawl her out and say that was no way to talk about my uncle George. That was one of Mom's favorite jokes and was probably the reason she allowed the dog to stay on the place. At least nobody ever thought of another reason.

I used to beg for a decent dog—a Labrador retriever, an Irish setter, or just a regular old mongrel like most of the other guys had—but with no success. We just weren't a two-dog family, and since no one in his right mind would take Strange and Mom wouldn't take advantage of anyone who revealed his low mentality by offering to take Strange, I was stuck with him.

Strange didn't even make good as a criminal. In our part of the country the worst crime a dog can commit is to run deer. As soon as Strange found this out, he rushed out into our clover field and tried to run the deer that grazed there. They would have none of it. They looked at the wildly yapping creature dancing around them and went back to their munching.

Strange had only two chores, but he could never get them straight. He was supposed to attack prowlers, especially those whose character bore the slightest resemblance to his own, and to protect the chickens. He always thought it was the other way around.

Whenever he was caught assaulting a chicken he would come up with some cock-and-bull story about how the chicken had been about to set fire to the house when he, Strange, happened along and prevented arson. "Bad enough we have a dog that attacks chickens, we have to have one that lies about it besides!" Mom would say. (It should be understood that Strange did not actually speak in words, or at least that anyone ever heard, but with his eyes and gestures with feet, tail, and ears.)

As for prowlers, Strange would go out and invite tramps in off the road for a free meal. While the dog was out in the yard apologizing to the tramp for my grandmother's cooking, the womenfolk would peek out through the curtains and try to determine whether the fellow was dangerous. If so, they would wait until he had just about finished his meal and then my sister would bellow, "Do you want the gun, Ma? Do you want the gun?" This usually would bring the tramp to his feet and send him at a fast walk toward the nearest cover, the ditch on the far side of the road. Even had the gun been real, which it wasn't, the tramp would have been in no danger—unless of course he happened to step between Mom and the dog.

As soon as I was old enough to hunt I would borrow a shotgun and sneak out to the woods in search of grouse. I had to sneak, not because Mom disapproved of my hunting, but because Strange would insist upon going along and contributing his advice and services. An army of Cossacks could have bivouacked on our front lawn for the night without his knowing a thing about it, but he could hear the sound of a shotgun shell being dropped into a flannel shirt pocket at a hundred yards.

Just as I would be easing my way out the door, he would come staggering out of the woodshed, his eyes bloodshot and bleary from a night of carousing, and say, "My suggestion is that we try Schultz's woods first and then work our way up Stagg's hill and if we don't get anything there we can stop by the Haversteads and shoot some of their chickens."

Strange made slightly less noise going through the woods than an armored division through a bamboo jungle. Nevertheless, we usually managed to get a few birds, apparently because they thought that anything that made that much noise couldn't possibly be hunting.

My dog believed in a mixed bag: grouse, ducks, pheasants, rabbits, squirrels, chipmunks, gophers, skunks, and porcupines. If we saw a cow or horse, he would shout, "There's a big one! Shoot! Shoot!"

Fortunately, Strange tired of hunting after about an hour. "Let's eat the lunch now," he would say. If he had been particularly disgusting that day, I would lie and tell him that I had forgotten to bring a lunch, knowing that it was against his principle—he only had one—to ever be caught more than an hour's distance away from a food supply. He would immediately strike off for home with the look of a man who has suddenly been deposited in the middle of the Mojave Desert.

Thus it went through most of the years of my youth, until finally Strange's years totaled what we supposed to be about a dozen. He sensed death approaching—probably the first thing in his life he ever did sense approaching—and one day staggered to a window, looked out and said, "A dog like me should live for a thousand years!" Then he died.

Everyone wept and said he hadn't been such a bad dog after all. Everyone except my grandmother, who simply smiled to herself as she stirred the gravy.

That night at dinner I said, "This sure is lumpy gravy," and "This pie crust sure is tough." It seemed the least I could do for Strange.

As I say, there was a time when I would have traded a dog like Strange in an instant for a mechanical bird dog. But now? Well, let me think about that for a while.

The Modified Stationary Panic

EVERY SO OFTEN I read an article on how to survive when lost in the wilds, and I have to laugh. The experts who write these pieces know everything about survival but next to nothing about getting lost. I am an expert on getting lost. I have been lost in nine different countries, forty-three cities, seven national forests, four national parks, countless parking lots, and one Amtrak passenger train. My wife claims I once got lost riding an elevator in a tall building, but that is an unwarranted exaggeration based on my momentary confusion over the absence of a thirteenth floor. (If you are a person with an inherent fear of heights, you want to make certain that all the floors are right where they are supposed to be, and you're not about to listen to a lot of lame excuses for any empty space between the twelfth and fourteenth floors.)

Since I have survived all of these experiences

of being lost, it follows that I am also something of an expert on survival. Consequently, out of my identification with and concern for that portion of humanity that frequently finds itself in the predicament of not knowing its way home from its left elbow, I have been motivated to publish the following compilation of field-tested tips on how to get lost. I have also included information on how to survive, and, of equal interest, how to pass the time if you don't.

The most common method for getting lost starts with telling a hunting partner, "I'll just cut down over the hill here and meet you on the first road." Nine times out of ten, the next road in the direction you choose is the Trans-Canada Highway. That is, of course, unless you are in Canada, in which case it may well be a supply route to a Siberian reindeer farm.

Another good method for getting lost in a quick and efficient manner is to rely on a companion who claims to have infallible sense of direction. Spin him around any time, any place in the world, according to him, and he will automatically point toward home. Your first clue that his sense of direction is somewhat overrated comes when he says something like, "Hey, now that's weird! The sun is setting in the east!" There is, of course, an appropriate response to such a statement. Unfortunately, it may result in a long jail term.

My favorite method for getting lost is daydreaming. I'll be trailing a deer whose tracks are so old pine seedlings will have sprouted in them. When I have to count the growth rings on a tree to determine how fresh a set of tracks is, my interest in the hunt begins to wane. Pretty soon I'm daydreaming. I imagine myself shooting a trophy buck. Then I unsheath my knife, dress him out, and drag him back to camp, where my hunting companions go wild with envy and astonishment.

"Would ya look at the size of that buck ol' Pat got!"

"Man, where did you ever get a beauty like that?"

"Just tracked him down," I say. "He was a smart one too, but every so often he made the mistake of bending a blade of grass the wrong way. The wind changed and spooked him though, and I had to drop him on a dead run at nine hundred yards and . . ."

And I'll look around and I'll be lost. The last time I had looked, I was hunting in a pine woods on a mountain. Now I'll be so deep in a swamp the wildlife is a couple of stages back on the scale of evolution. (It's bad enough being lost without having to put up with a bunch of feathered lizards learning to fly.)

Undoubtedly, the surest way to get lost is to venture into the woods as a member of a group. Sooner or later one of the boys, on a pretext of offering up a riddle, says, "Hey, guys, I bet none of you can tell me which direction the car is in. Heh heh." (The "heh heh" is tacked on to imply that he knows the right direction, but truth is he couldn't tell it from a kidney stone.) Everyone now points firmly and with great authority in a different direction. In every such case, the most forceful personality in the group gets his way. The effectiveness of this method arises out of the fact that the most forceful personality usually turns out to rank on intelligence scales somewhere between sage hens and bowling balls. He is also an accomplished magician. With a wave of his arm and the magic words "the car's just over that next rise" he can make the whole bunch of you vanish for three days.

While the process of becoming lost is usually a lot of fun, the entertainment value diminishes rapidly once the act is accomplished. The first small twinges of fear, however, do not last long, and are soon replaced by waves of terror. There is also a sense of general disorientation, the first symptom of which is confusion about which side of your head your face is on. Two questions immediately occur to the lost outdoorsman: "What shall I do now?" and "Why didn't I stick with golf?"

I disagree sharply with most survival experts on what the lost person should do first. Most of them start out by saying some fool thing like, "The first rule of survival is DON'T PANIC!" Well, anyone who has ever been lost knows that kind of advice is complete nonsense. They might as well tell you "DON'T SWEAT!" or "DON'T GET GOOSE BUMPS ALL OVER YOUR BODY!"

Survival experts are apparently such calm, rational people themselves that they assume a lost person spends considerable time deliberating the question of whether he should panic: "Let's see, the first thing I'll do is panic, and then I'll check to see on which side of the trees the moss is growing." It doesn't work that way.

First of all, one is either a panicker or one isn't, and the occasion of being lost is no time to start fretting about a flaw in one's character. My own theory holds that it is best, if one is a panicker, to get the panic out of the system as quickly as possible. Holding panic in may cause severe psychological disorders and even stomach cramps and baldness. Also, the impacted panic may break loose at a later date, if there is a later date, and cause one to sprint across a shopping mall yelling "Help! Help!" at the top of his lungs. Shopping malls being what they are, no one would probably notice but it might be embarrassing anyway.

Over the years I've been involved in several dozen panics, usually as a participant, sometimes simply as an observer. Most of my panics have been of a solitary nature, but on several occasions I have organized and led group panics, one of which involved twenty-some people. In that instance a utility company took advantage of the swath we cut through the forest and built a power line along it.

Back in the earlier days of my panicking I utilized what is known technically as the Full Bore Linear Panic (FBLP). This is where you run flat out in a straight line until the course of your panic is deflected by a large rock or tree, after which you get up and sprint off in the new direction. The FBLP is also popularly referred to as the ricochet or pinball panic or sometimes simply as "going bananas." Once an FBLP is underway there is no stopping it. It gains momentum at every stride, and the participants get so caught up in it they forget the reason for holding it in the first place. They'll panic right out of the woods, onto a road, down the road, through a town, and back into the woods, all the time picking up momentum. One time when we were kids my friend Retch and I panicked right through a logging crew and the loggers dropped what they were doing and ran along with us under the impression we were being pursued by something. When they found out all we were doing was panicking, they fell back, cursing, and returned to their work. This tendency of panic to feed upon itself gives it ever-increasing momentum and occasionally indigestion.

Although it will do absolutely no good, I must advise against undertaking a Full Bore Linear Panic unless, of course, one is equipped with a stout heart, a three-day supply of food, and a valid passport. Instead, I recommend the Stationary or Modified Panic. It offers the same therapeutic effect and subsides after a few minutes with none of the FBLP's adverse side effects, such as making your life insurance company break out in a bad rash.

The Stationary Panic first came to my attention one time when a large but harmless snake slithered across a trail a couple of yards ahead of my wife. She made a high-pitched chittering sound and began jumping up and down and flailing the air with her arms. It was a most impressive performance, particularly since each jump was approximately a foot high and her backpack happened to be the one with the tent on it. The only adverse side effect to the Stationary Panic was that the lone witness to the spectacle could not help laughing every time he thought about it, a reaction quickly remedied, however, by his sleeping most of the night outside the tent in a driving rainstorm.

Although I immediately perceived the advantage of this form of panic, I could not imagine myself bouncing up and down, flailing my arms and chittering like an angry squirrel, particularly in front of the rough company with whom I usually find myself in a predicament requiring a panic. Thus it came about that I invented the Modified Stationary Panic, or MSP.

The key to the MSP is not to bounce up and down in a monotonous fashion but to vary the steps so that it appears to be a sort of folk dance. You can make up your own steps but I highly recommend throwing in a couple of Russian squat kicks. The chittering sound should be replaced by an Austrian drinking song, shouted out at the top of your voice. The MSP is particularly appropriate for group panics. There are few sights so inspiring as a group of lost hunters, arms entwined, dancing and singing for all they are worth as night closes in upon them.

Once you have established the fact that you are

indeed lost and have performed the perfunctory Modified Panic, you should get started right away on the business of surviving. Many survival experts recommend that you first determine on which side of the trees the moss is growing. I'm not sure why this is, but I suppose it it because by the time you get hungry enough to eat moss you will want to know where to find it in a hurry.

If you think you may have to spend the night in the woods, you may wish to fashion some form of temporary shelter. For one night, a tree with good thick foliage will serve the purpose. Thick foliage will help keep the rain off, and reduces the chance of falling out of the tree.

After a day or two, it is probably a good idea to build a more permanent shelter, such as a lean-to. A very nice lean-to can be made out of large slabs of bark, pried from a dead cedar, pine or tamarack, and leaned against the trunk of an upright tree. If you have a tendency to walk in your sleep, the lean-to should not be more than fifteen feet from the ground. After a couple of weeks, it might be a good idea to add some simple furnishings and pictures.

Each day you are lost should be recorded by carving a notch on some handy surface. (This procedure should be skipped by anyone lost at sea in a rubber life raft.) I've known people lost only a few hours and already they had carved half a notch. The reason for the notches is that you may write a book on your experience and sell it to the movies. As is well known, a film about being lost is absolute zilch without an ever-increasing string of notches. The best film treatment of notches that I've seen was in a TV movie about a couple whose plane had crashed in the Yukon. They painted the notches on the plane's fuselage with a set of oil paints. It was a great touch and added a lot of color to the drama. I for one never go out into the woods anymore without a set of oil paints, just in case I'm lucky enough to be lost long enough to interest a film producer.

Many survival experts are of the opinion that lost persons have little to fear from wild animals. I disagree. It is true that bear and cougar will almost always do their best to avoid contact with human beings, but how about squirrels and grouse? On several occasions the sound of a squirrel charging through dry leaves has inflicted partial paralysis on my upper ganglia, erasing from my consciousness the knowledge that one has nothing to fear from bear or cougar. Having a grouse blast off from under one's feet can cause permanent damage to one's psyche. The first-aid recommended for restoring vital bodily functions after such occurrences is simply to pound your chest several times with a large rock. On the other hand, if the jolt has been sufficient to lock your eyelids in an open position, it is best to leave them that way. This will prevent you from dozing off during the night and falling out of your tree.

The excitement of being lost wears off rather quickly, and after a few days boredom sets in. It is then that one may wish to turn to some of the proven techniques for getting one's self found. Building a large smoky fire is always good. During fire season, this will almost always attract attention and it won't be long before a team of smoke-jumpers will be parachuted in to put out the fire. They may be a little angry about having their poker game back at camp interrupted but can usually be persuaded to take you out of the woods with them anyway. (The term "survival tip," by the way, originated from the practice of giving smoke-jumpers five dollars each for not leaving the fire-builder behind.) There is always the possibility that a bomber may just fly over and dump a load of fire retardant on you and your fire and you will have to turn to other measures.

Scooping water up in your hat and pouring it down a badger hole is good, if you are fortunate enough to have both a hat and a badger hole handy. Someone is bound to show up to ask you why you are doing such a fool thing. If this person isn't afraid of associating with a madman, he will probably show you the way home.

Similarly, you can try your hand at catching some large fish. If you're successful, three anglers will immediately emerge from the brush and ask you what bait you're using. In case you don't have a valid fishing license, one of the three will be a game warden who will place you under arrest as soon as he has caught his own limit. But at least you'll be found.

When everything else fails and you are really desperate, you can always resort to taking off all your clothes. Even when lost, I've never known this technique to fail in attracting a large crowd of people, no matter how far back in the wilderness I happened to be. Here's an example:

My friend Retch and I had been fishing a high mountain stream at least three miles from the nearest road.

We hadn't seen a sign of human life all day. The fish had stopped biting and we were hot and sticky and decided to take a dip in a pool beneath a small waterfall.

We took off our clothes and dove into the water, the temperature of which instantly proved to be somewhere between damn cold and ice. As we popped to the surface, and started flailing wildly toward the ledge from which we had dived, approximately twelve members of a mushroom club rounded a bend in the trail and headed straight for us. I would like to be able to tell you that modesty forced us to remain submerged in that liquid ice until they had passed, their pleasant outing unblemished by nothing more lascivious than a patch of morel mushrooms. Unfortunately, that would not be the truth. The startling spectacle of two grown men lunging out of the water, snatching up their clothes and racing off through a thicket of devil's club was at least mitigated by the fact that most of the ladies in the group apparently thought we were wearing blue leotards. I was also relieved that a particularly bad twelve-letter word had frozen on Retch's lower lip and didn't thaw out until we were in the car driving home.

Perhaps the most important thing to remember when lost is to accept the experience in a philosophical manner. Whenever I start becoming slightly confused over which is my elbow and which the way home and night is tightening its noose upon me in some primordial swamp, I never fail to recall the folksy wisdom spoken to me under similar circumstances by the old woodsman Rancid Crabtree. Rancid spat out his chaw of tobacco and in that comical, bug-eyed way of his said, "JUMPIN' GOSH ALMIGHTY, WHERE IN HELL IS WE?!" Somehow those words always seem a fitting introduction to a lively folk dance and a rousing rendition of an Austrian drinking song.

Grogan's War Surplus

My OLD CAMPING BUDDY Retch, his eyes dreamy and wet with nostalgia, leaned forward and stirred the fire under our sizzling pan of trout with a stick. I could tell he was getting deep into his cups because that's the only time he turns sloppily sentimental. Also, we were cooking on a propane camp stove.

"You know," he said, "it seems like only yesterday that you and me was crouched in the mud in some Godforsaken place using our bayonets to roast a couple hunks of Spam over some canned heat."

"Yeah, and heatin' our water in a steel helmet," I said, sinking suddenly into the morass of reminiscence. "And lyin' awake night after night in a pup tent, listenin' for the first sound of attack . . ."

". . . and half our gear riddled with bullet holes," Retch put in, shaking a tear off the end of his mustache.

"Yep," I said, "we really had some great campin'

when we were kids. It's just too damn bad kids nowadays don't have some of those old-time war surplus stores around to sell them their campin' gear."

Retch forked a small, crisp trout out of the pan and munched it down tail first. "Say, what was it that was always attackin' us in those days?"

"I'm not sure what they were called," I said, glancing out into the surrounding darkness, "but they were always big and hairy and had red eyes, and teeth the size of railroad spikes. I haven't seen one of them since I was twelve years old." I leaned over and stopped Retch from throwing a log on the fire. "Not when I was sober, anyway."

"Say," Retch said suddenly. "You remember ol' Grogan's War Surplus store?"

Did I remember Grogan's War Surplus store! Why, the mere sound of that melodious name made my heart dance the Light Fantastic. Grogan's War Surplus. Ah, how could I ever forget!

Immediately after World War II, Grogan had remodeled an old livery stable and feed store in the style now referred to in architectural textbooks as "war surplus modern," a decor that attempts to emulate the aesthetic effects of a direct hit on an army ordnance depot.

The store front itself was elegantly festooned with gerry cans, yellow life rafts, landing nets, ammo boxes, and other assorted residue of recent history. On the lot behind the store, the plundered wreckage of a dozen or so military vehicles had been cleverly arranged in such a manner as to conceal what had once been an unsightly patch of wild flowers. But all the really precious stuff was kept inside the store itself, illuminated by a few naked light bulbs and the watchful eyes of Henry P. Grogan.

The great thing about Grogan's War Surplus

was not only did it sell every conceivable thing that might possibly be used for camping, but it was cheap. With a few dollars and a sharp eye for a bargain, you could go into Grogan's and outfit yourself with at least the bare essentials for the routine overnight camping trip—a sleeping bag, pup tent, canteen, cook kit, entrenching shovel, paratrooper jump boots, leggings, packboard, packsack, web belt, ammo pouches, medic kit, machete, bayonet, steel helmet, fiber helmet liner, .45 automatic holster (empty), G.I. can opener, and the other basic necessities.

Then if you had any change left, you might pick up a few luxury items, things you had no idea what they might be used for but were reasonably sure you would think of something—ammo box, camouflage net, G.I. soap, parachute harness, and the like.

Naturally, you never took all of this gear with you on a simple overnight trip. Nine times out of ten you forgot the soap and probably the can opener, too.

Since one of the rules of backpacking requires that all nonessentials be omitted from the pack, we strained our imaginations to bring every last piece of beloved war surplus into the realm of our necessities.

Take the bayonet, for example. It was needed for cutting and spearing things. Frequently, it cut and speared things we didn't want cut and speared, but this drawback was more than made up for by its otherwise benign service as a cooking spit, paring knife, or even use as a tent stake.

The machete was needed anytime you had to slash out your own trail. This necessity arose more often than a person who is not a kid with a machete might think. Sometimes you had to walk several miles out of your way in order for that particular necessity to arise but time was of no consequence when you were in search of necessity. Over the years we slashed out literally hundreds of trails through the wilderness. The longest of these was The Great Rocky Mountain Divide Trail. It was never used much by backpackers, but the mother of a friend of mine, who lived at the jumping-off point, later put up a post at each end of the trail and strung a clothesline between them. The other trails we built, of course, were not nearly so impressive as this one.

We had learned from war movies that steel helmets could be used for boiling things in. On hot summer days, we found out what—our heads. The helmets could also be used for pillows. If you went to sleep, your head would slip off the helmet and bonk on the ground. Bonking your boiled head on the ground kept you awake all night, which was one of the reasons for using a helmet for a pillow in the first place.

Filling up a .45 automatic holster was always a challenge, particularly since our parents had indicated they would just as soon we didn't buy any .45 automatics. About the only thing you could do with the holster was stuff a sardine-cheese-pickle-onion sandwich in it to be quickdrawn anytime you got hungry. Actually, a .45 automatic probably would have been safer than some of our sandwiches.

You had to be a shrewd shopper not to get taken by Henry P. Grogan. We realized that some of the war surplus was brand-spanking-new. Other merchandise had obviously seen combat; it was cracked, tarnished, stained, ripped, riddled, rotten, rusty, and moldy. Frequently, Henry P. would try to pawn off some of the new stuff on us but we weren't to be fooled. We held out for the authentic war surplus. Ah, you can't imagine how old Henry P. would roll his eyes and gnash his teeth every time one of us kids outwitted him like that. He'd get very angry.

The real treasure, of course, was any item with a bullet hole in it. For a long time you practically never came across anything with a bullet hole in it, and then one day Larry Swartze found a canteen with what looked like an honest-to-goodness bullet hole drilled through it. Henry P. himself had to break up the fight to see who was going to get the perforated canteen. Immediately after that incident, all sorts of war surplus turned up with bullet holes in it, and we kept ourselves broke trying to buy it all. Then it occurred to us that maybe old Henry P. was going around at night with a hammer and large spike, counterfeiting bullet holes. The bottom subsequently dropped out of the bullet-hole market at Henry P's.

Shrewd as I was, Henry P. managed to take even me a few times. One of the worst things he did was to sell me what he called "one of the down bags used by Arctic troops to keep them comfortable in 70-below weather." The bags turned out to be a secret weapon of the War Department, designed to be dropped behind the lines in hopes that enemy troops would attempt to sleep in them and either freeze or break out in an itch that would occupy both hands scratching for the duration of the war. The stuffing consisted not of down but chicken feathers with, if the size of the lumps in the bag was any indication, several of the chickens still attached. But the worst feature of the bag was triggered by its getting even slightly wet. Any time it rained on one of our camping trips, I went home smelling like high tide at the local chicken and turkey farm.

Another time, Henry P. induced me to buy a

two-man mountain tent, so called, I later discovered, because it was heavy as a mountain and took two men to set it up. The roof of the tent looked like it had been made out of dried batskin, and was impervious to everything but wind, rain, and heavy dew. A tubular air vent extended from each end of the tent, an effect which, combined with the batskin roof, gave it the appearance of a creature dropped in from outer space. It frequently gave us quite a start when we returned to camp late in the evening and glimpsed the pterodactylous wings of the roof flapping in the breeze and the vent tubes bobbing about. I remember one occasion when a brave kid named Kenny stood at a distance and threw rocks, trying to drive our tent out of camp.

The tent was designed to sleep two grown men, providing they were both Pygmies and on exceptionally good terms with each other. We managed to crowd four of us into it, after drawing straws to see who got to have their heads by the air vents. The losers had to suck their air through bullet holes. If a loud sound suddenly reminded us of unfinished business at home, there was always a big traffic jam at the exit. Sometimes we would be about halfway home and still not out of the tent yet.

As a result of these drawbacks to the mountain tent, I was constantly on the lookout for some kind of portable shelter that would afford me a bit more comfort and protection. One day, poking around Grogan's War Surplus, I found it. After sorting through the ever-present snarl of nylon rope, I discovered a canvas tube attached to dried batskin and mosquito netting. The mosquito netting on one side had a zipper running the full length of it.

"What is it?" I asked Grogan.

"That, my boy, is a jungle hammock," he said. "This canvas is the hammock part, the mosquito netting is the walls, and then this tough and very attractive fabric here is the roof."

Not having any jungles readily available, I inquired as to how it would work in our part of the world.

"Just fine," he said. "For example, there's some folks who don't much care for slimy, crawly ol' snakes sneakin' into their nice, cozy 70-below down sleepin' bags to get warm, and they like this here jungle hammock because it keeps 'em outta reach of the poisonous critters."

I didn't let on in the slightest to Grogan that he had just made reference to my kind of people. He nevertheless came to that conclusion because he scooped up the jungle hammock and carried it toward the checkout counter.

"How is it for bears?" I asked in a tone of complete indifference, following along behind him.

"Bears? Oh, it's fine on bears. In bear country you just hitch it a little higher in the trees—say, about fifteen feet."

The roof of the jungle hammock had some bad cracks in it, several of the ropes were frayed, the mosquito netting had small tears in it, and the canvas looked as if it were being attacked by at least four varieties of exotic mold. Grogan didn't seem to notice though and let me have it for not much more than he would have charged for a new one.

I lost no time in getting the jungle hammock home and suspended between two trees in our backyard for a trial run. It looked so secure suspended up there in the air—a modest ten feet from the ground—that I decided I would spend the night there.

The family came out that evening to cheer me on as I climbed the stepladder to launch myself on my maiden voyage in the hammock. After they had retreated back into the house, muttering enviously I thought, I zipped up the mosquito netting, wiggled into my chicken-down sleeping bag, and lay back to contemplate the closing in of my ancient enemy, darkness.

After four or five hours of this contemplation, an unnerving thought occurred to me. I had not remembered to have the stepladder removed! It continued to connect ground and hammock like a boarding ramp for any ravenous beast that happened along. I leaned over to kick the ladder. As I did so the hammock flipped on its side, sending me like a shot through the mosquito netting, still encased in my sleeping bag.

As bad luck would have it, my crotchety old dog, Strange, had a short while before staggered in from a night of carousing and collapsed on the target area. Nothing in his experience, of course, had taught him to expect me even to be out at night let alone suspended in the air ten feet above him. Consequently, when a large, screeching shape wrapped in chicken feathers plummeted down on him out of the darkness, it was certainly reasonable for him to assume that he had fallen prey to some huge, carnivorous bird of the night. I, for my part, fully expected to be greeted by a hairy beast with fast, snapping jaws, an expectation that did not go unfulfilled. Within ten seconds we had fought ourselves to a state of total exhaustion, perhaps not surprising when you consider the fact that we had gone fully around the yard three times, failed in our attempts to climb several trees and a lilac bush, battered open the door to the house, and finally collapsed in a single panting heap on the kitchen floor. Both of us smelled of wet chicken feathers for days afterwards, and it was a full week before I could brush the taste of dog off my teeth.

After I had recovered from that night though, I couldn't help chuckling over how I had put one over on ol' Grogan. If Henry P. had known the mosquito netting on that jungle hammock was eaten plumb through with jungle rot he would have charged me twice the price that he did.

"Do I remember Henry P. Grogan's War Surplus store?" I said to Retch. "Wasn't his that high-class place with the sign that said SHIRTS AND SHOES MUST BE WORN ON THESE PREMISES?"

But he didn't hear me. He was too busy blowing on the fire.

The Big Trip

WHEN I WAS VERY YOUNG and the strange wild passion for mountains was first upon me, I wrote, produced, and directed for myself a magnificent, colossal, 3-D, Technicolor, Wide-Screen, Stereophonic fantasy—the fantasy of the Big Trip.

Whenever the jaws of tedium gnawed too harshly on my bones, I simply turned down the lights on the murk and grind of the world outside and projected the fantasy on the backsides of my eyeballs, each of which was equipped with a Silver Screen.

The fantasy was primarily an adventure story set in the vast wilderness of the Selkirk mountains. It starred You Know Whom, who bore a striking resemblance to a four-foot-eight-inch Gregory Peck. The basic plot was that the hero, a pack on his back, hiked far back into these beautiful mountains, endured great hardships, overcame terrible obstacles, and occasionally even rescued from perilous distress a beautiful red-haired lady. It was strictly a G-rated fantasy. (The R- and X-rated fantasies came later.) But I enjoyed it. In fact, with time, the Big Trip began to gain a strange sort of dominance over my life.

Several times the fantasy prevented my perishing from a loathsome childhood affliction: school. Once in a seventh-grade English class I stumbled into a nest of dangling participles. Had I not been able to get my fantasy going in time, those slimy, leechlike creatures would have drained me dry as a puffball in five minutes.

On occasion, Mr. Rumsdale, our seventh-grade English teacher, would unexpectedly break through the thick and buttressed walls of our indifference and start throwing parts of speech in all directions. Several of my friends were knocked silly by flying objects of the preposition, but long before there was any threat to my own cherished ignorance, the old fantasy would carry me to safety. I would be roasting a fresh-caught trout on the rocky shore of some high and distant stream, or maybe just striding along under the sweet weight of a good pack, and it would be morning in the mountains, with the sun rising through the trees.

Mr. Rumsdale once lowered the battering ram he used for a voice and told me that I had better stop this constant dreaming. Otherwise, he predicted, both he and I would probably die as old men in seventh-grade English.

Even I knew by then that the Big Trip, for all its utility as an antidote to boredom, could not endure forever simply as fantasy. One day I would have to turn it into the real thing. I would have to take the Big Trip back into the mountains and face great hardship and overcome terrible obstacles. To that end, I began serving an apprenticeship in the out-of-doors.

I practiced "sleeping out alone" in the backyard, my ears ever alert to the approaching footpad of some hairy terror, until at last I conquered my over-powering fear of the dark and the ghastly things that flourished there. I learned to build fires, using nothing more than a few sticks, a couple of newspapers, and a box and a half of kitchen matches. I studied the art of camp cookery, and soon could serve up a hearty meal of flaming bacon, charred potatoes, three-pound pancakes, and butterscotch pudding with gnat topping. After a longer time, I even taught myself to eat these things. Through practical experience, I learned that it is best not to dry wet boots over a fire with your feet still in them. I learned that some sleeping bags are stuffed with the same filler used in dynamite fuse and that it is best not to let sparks land on one of them, particularly when it is occupied by your body. Thus did the Big Trip shape my life and give meaning even to its failures and disasters.

As I grew older, I went off with friends on numerous lengthy trips into the mountains, thinking each time that perhaps at last I was making the Big Trip. But I never was. These were pleasant, amiable excursions, occasionally distinguished by a crisis or two, but I was always disappointed by the realization that they fell far short of the Big Trip of my aging fantasy. So one day in the summer that I turned seventeen, I decided I would at last, once and for all, plan and exe-cute, or be executed by, the Big Trip.

When I announced and elaborated on my plans for the benefit of my mother and stepfather, there was great wailing and a gnashing of teeth already well gnashed from my previous and much lesser excursions into the wilderness. From then until the day I left, my mother could scarcely take time out from climbing the walls to make the beds and cook our meals.

The plans were indeed formidable, and in my

unsure moments they even caused me to wail and gnash a little. The terrain I planned to cross looked on a topographical map like the scribblings of a mildly demented chimpanzee and spanned a distance of some thirty miles as the crow flies. If the crow walked, as they say, it was more like fifty. The area was unmarred by roads or trails. It contained plenty of tracks, though, some of which belonged to grizzlies. And as everyone knows, a grizzly, if he happens along at the right moment, can transform a quiet walk to a privy into a memorable experience.

Preparations for the Big Trip were remarkably simple, since by this time I knew that nothing destroys a Big Trip quicker than a surplus of comforts or a dearth of hardships. And a Big Trip is defined by its hardships.

These hardships, of course, could not be left to mere chance. A number of them had to be prepared in advance and taken along in the pack, so to speak, to be trotted out any time the going got easy. The basic formula for creating hardships is to take no nonessentials and only a few of the essentials.

One of the essentials you leave behind is most of the food. My stock of grub consisted of pancake flour, a slab of bacon, dried fruit, butter, sugar, and salt. For emergency rations, I took a bag of dehydrated chicken noodle soup, enough, it turned out, to feed an army of starving Cossacks for upwards of three weeks.

About the only gear I took was a sleeping bag, a knife, and a rifle. I carried along the rifle in case I ran into a grizzly, since my idea of hardships did not include getting eaten by a bear. Although I knew a .32 Special couldn't stop a charging grizzly, I took comfort in the notion that I might be able to take the edge off his appetite on his way to the table. In the early days of my fantasy, I had conceived of building a stockade each night as protection against bears, but when you have a grizzly coming for you, no matter how much encouragement and incentive he might offer, it is difficult to get a stockade up in time to do much good. So I was taking the rifle.

At practically the last moment, I decided to take along a companion. In light of the other meticulous preparations for the Big Trip, it seems incongruous now that I should have selected my traveling companion so casually. Retch, as he will be known here, had just moved to town recently and was probably the only person of my acquaintance who had not heard of the Big Trip. This gap in his knowledge may be the reason that he was the only person I could find who was ready and willing to accompany me on the expedition. Perhaps in my last-minute desperation for companionship I skipped a few details and did not impress upon him the full magnitude of the trip.

"How would you like to go on a camping trip?" I asked him. "Spend a few days hiking around in the mountains, catch some fish, cook out?"

Retch said he thought he would like that. Somehow he got the impression we were going on an extended fishing trip and marshmallow roast. Later, under somewhat harsher circumstances, he was to reveal to me that never in his whole life had he nourished any fantasies about a Big Trip. I was appalled that a human life could be so sterile, so devoid of splendor.

Even by the time my parents were driving us to the jumping-off spot, Retch still did not fully comprehend the full portent of the Big Trip. My stepfather's funereal air, my mother's quivering lips, and my own grim silence, however, began to undermine his confidence.

"It isn't as though we're going to be gone for-

ever," he would say, attempting to console my mother.
She would reply with a low, quavering moan. By the
time we disembarked from the car, Retch was convinced
that we were going to be gone forever.

As things turned out, he was nearly right.

For two pleasant days, the Big Trip did seem
as if it were going to be nothing more than an ordinary
camping trip, and therefore not a Big Trip at all. The
sky was an impeccable blue, the firewood dry and
fragrant, the trout in the lakes fat and hungry, the
huckleberries sweet. I could scarcely conceal my disap-
pointment at the good time we were having.

On the third morning I was awakened by a
howl of anguish from Retch. "The deer got into our
packs and ate everything but the bacon and chicken
noodle soup," he yelled.

My heart laughed up. This, finally, was a real
hardship.

"Don't worry," I said. "We can always live off
the country." Then I looked around. The country didn't
seem to be very edible. Perhaps the trip would be
harder than even I expected.

Later that same day, we came across what we
thought must be fresh grizzly tracks. Concluding that
where there are fresh grizzly tracks, there are likely to
be fresh grizzlies, we quickened our pace. Near the top
of the next mountain, we slowed to a dogtrot, which we
maintained for the rest of the day.

That night we camped on a barren ridge without water, and ate fried bacon and soup for supper. The
soup, which wasn't much good with water, was even
worse without it. (The fact that the deer had not
touched the chicken noodle soup proved to me once
and for all that deer are animals of good sense and dis-
criminating taste.) After dinner, we sat around the fire
picking the bacon out of our teeth with noodles.

"I've got an idea," Retch said.

"What?" I said.

"Let's quit," he said.

Our quitting then would have been like a sky-diver's quitting halfway to the ground. "Don't worry," I said. "It will be a lot easier from now on."

Storm clouds were rising in the west when we crawled into our sleeping bags. Soon the heavy, black thunderheads were over us. Lightning licked the peak of our mountain a few times and then started walking down the ridge toward us. When it struck close enough to bounce us off the ground, I predicted, breathlessly, "It's going to pass over the top of us. Next time it will strike down below . . ."

By the time I was this far along in my prophecy, it was evident that I didn't have much future as a prophet. It didn't seem as if I even had much future.

When you see lightning hit from a distance, it appears that the bolt zaps into the ground and that's it, but when you are occupying the ground the bolt zaps into, it's not that way at all. First, a terrible bomb goes off and you're inside the bomb, and then streams of fire are going every which way and you're going every which way, and the brush lights up like neon signs in China-town, and there are pools of fire on the ground and high voltage sings in the air. Then it's dark again, black, sticky dark, and the rain hits like a truckful of ice.

The first thing I noticed, upon regaining consciousness, was that I was running to beat hell down the side of the mountain. I was wearing only my shorts. I do not know if I was fully dressed or not when the lightning hit.

Something was bounding like a deer through the brush ahead of me, and I hoped it was a deer and not a grizzly, because I was gaining on it. Then I saw that it was just a pair of white shorts, or reasonably white shorts, also running down the mountain. I yelled at the white shorts that I thought there was a cliff up ahead. The white shorts gave a loud yelp and vanished.

I found Retch sorting and counting his bones at the bottom end of a ten-foot drop. He said he might have been hurt worse, but some rocks cushioned his fall.

"You didn't happen to bring an aspirin, did you?" he said.

"No," I said.

"I didn't think so," he said.

While we were draining out sleeping bags (it was raining, remember), I made one last attempt at prophecy.

"Well, Retch," I said, "think of it this way—things just can't get any worse than they are right now."

In the days that followed we were to look back upon that moment as a time of great good fortune and decadent high living.

The driving, ice-cold rain continued through the night. The next morning we crawled out of our sleeping bags, stirred around in the mud until we found our clothes, put them on, and with an absolute minimum of jovial banter, spent an unsuccessful hour trying to start a fire. For breakfast we stirred up some chicken noodle soup in muddy water. The muddy water improved the flavor and texture of the soup considerably, and by drinking it through our teeth we could strain out the larger pebbles and even some of the noodles.

On all sides of us, as far as a bloodshot eye could see, was a vast, raging storm of mountains. Our soggy map told us we were ten miles from the end of the nearest trail, more than twenty miles from the nearest road. Retch and I stared at each other across the pile of steaming sticks that represented our aborted effort at fire-building, and I could see a reflection of my own misery and despair swirling in his eyes. "What do we do now?" I thought.

Then I remembered a sure-fire remedy for predicaments of this sort. It was recommended to me by a fierce, old man who knew the mountains well and knew what they can do to a person. "When everything else has failed, there is only one thing to do," he said. "You tough it out."

So that is what we did. We toughed it out. We went down mountains, up mountains, around mountains, lunged over windfalls, through swamps, across rainswollen streams, and we ate handfuls of chicken noodle mush, and then surged on across more mountains, streams, and windfalls. Had we run across a grizzly we would have eaten him raw on the spot and strung his claws for necklaces. There was nothing now, perhaps not even a beautiful red-haired lady in perilous distress, that could have interrupted our relentless march.

And then one day—or was it night?—we walked out of the mountains. There were cars going by on the highway, people zipping comfortably along through their lives at a mile a minute, looking out at us in mild amusement and wondering what muddy, bloody fools were these. We had triumphed over the mountains and over ourselves and over the Big Trip, but nobody knew or cared what we had done. We limped along the road in search of a farmhouse with a phone, our clothes torn, bodies aching, jaws clenched on the bullet, and the last dehydrated chicken noodle soup we would ever eat in our lives still matting our wispy beards.

Then I heard a strange, small sound in the

empty air. I glanced over at Retch to see if he heard it too, and he did, and there was this little pained smile on his cracked lips. As we slogged along the sound grew in volume, swelling up and filling the silence and emptiness, until it reached a great thundering crescendo.

It was the sound of applause and cheering— the sound of a standing ovation.

The Theory and Application of Old Men

EVERY KID SHOULD HAVE an old man. I don't mean just a father. Fathers are all right and I'm not knocking them, since I'm one myself, but from a kid's point of view they spend entirely too much time at a thing called the office or some other equally boring place of work. If you're a kid, what you need is someone who can take you out hunting or fishing or just poking around in the woods anytime you feel the urge. That's an old man. Doing things like that is what old men were designed for.

If you've never had an old man of your own before, you may not know what to look for or how to use one once you find him. I am something of an expert on the subject, having studied under some of the best old men in the business. Someday I hope to get into the field myself. In any case, I am eminently qualified to advise you on getting and caring for your first old man.

First off, let us consider the problem of identifying old men in the field. All old men are male. This is important to remember, and even then one can make a mistake. Occasionally, on hunting trips I have discovered that what I thought were men turned out to be old women. Had they turned out to be young women, I would have been a good deal less disappointed, but that turn of circumstance almost never happens to me.

Here is a good basic description of an old man: He is a male person with white hair, a stubbly beard, wrinkled hide, bifocals, long underwear, chewing tobacco, and the disposition of a bull walrus with a bad case of the shingles. If you find a female person with these basic characteristics, she would probably work just as well.

Old men come in various vintages. The sixties are good, the seventies are excellent, and the eighties are prime. Nineties are fine too, but there is always the risk they won't make it to the punchline on a good story.

Every youngster should be properly trained in the safe handling of an old man before he is allowed to take one out alone. One good bit of advice is to treat every old man as if he were loaded. If a kid accidentally triggers an old man, he is liable to get his vocabulary peppered with colorful expressions that will send his mother into shock the first time one tumbles off his tender lips. As a boy, I once addressed a piece of malfunctioning machinery in the appropriately descriptive language of my own old man. Quick as lightning my grandmother struck, deftly boxing my ears in a one-two combination. Fortunately for me, she used a small box.

"You been hangin' out with that blinkety-blank old Rancid Crabtree agin," she said. "He jist ain't the sort for a blinkety-blank young boy always to be traipsin' after, and I'll tell him so next time I lay eyes on the blinkety-blank!" ("Blinkety-blank," by the way, was one of Mr. Crabtree's favorite words.) The very next time the old man was in our kitchen, ol' Gram lit into him, and he grinned like a shaggy old dog, sitting there dunking a big sugar cookie in his coffee. He was very good at concealing his fear of Gram.

Mr. Crabtree, by the way, had a definite aura about him, a presence that seemed to linger on in the house long after he had gone home. Frequently, my mother would comment on it. "Throw open the windows!" she would shout.

Let us next consider the proper technique for starting an old man. When you are older, you can start an old man simply by loading him or, in the more common expression, "getting him loaded." While you're still a kid, however, you will have to use empty old men, who are a good deal harder to start. The best technique for starting an empty old man is called "priming." You say something like this to your O.M.: "Mr. Jenkins, I'll bet fishing is sure a lot better nowadays than when you were a kid." That bit of priming should not only get him started but keep him going for a couple of hours.

A kid may come across an old man who gambles, drinks, lies, cusses, chews 'n' spits, and hates to shave and take baths, but there's also a chance that he will run into one with a lot of bad habits. There are two kinds of old men in particular that he wants to watch out for—the Sleeper and the Drifter.

Once you've gone to all the trouble of getting the Sleeper started, he will set you up something like this:

"So, that ol' sow b'ar shooshes her cubs up a tree, an' then she comes fer me. I can see she's got her heart set on turnin' my bride into a widder woman. Wall, I ups with my twenty-two single-shot . . ."

"Yes, yes?" you say. "Go on."

"Snort, mimph, wheeze, snore," he says. Sleepers will drop off like that every time, and you want to avoid them like the plague.

The Drifter is just as bad as the Sleeper and maybe even worse. Keep in mind that most old men are masters of the art of digression. They will start off something like this: "I recollect the time a bobcat got loose in Poke Martin's plane. Funniest thing I ever seen! Ol' Poke, he was flyin' supplies into Pat Doyle's camp at Terrible Crick—Terrible Crick, that's whar I caught a twenty-pound char one time on a piece of bacon rind. Ha! Ol' Shorty Long an' me was runnin' a trapline that winter, about the coldest winter since I got my tongue stuck on the pump handle when I was a youngun. Back in those days . . ." In this fashion the average old man will digress back to about the time the earth's crust was beginning to harden and then will work his way back to the original topic, touching every base as he goes. A brief anecdote is somehow transformed into the history of western civilization, but it is all entertaining and enlightening. The Drifter, however, just leaves you back there in the mists of time, the two of you looking about, wondering what it was you had come for.

"But what about the bobcat?" you ask, hoping to jog the Drifter's memory.

"Bobcat?" he says. "What bobcat?"

My own luck with old men over the years has been exceptionally good. I still keep a stable of them around to remind me of a time when men (and women, too) were measured not by whether their look was wet or dry but whether they possessed a mysterious quality called "grit." When I was a youngster, grit was the chief remedy for a variety of ailments. "What that boy needs," an old man would prescribe, "is more grit." A deficiency in grit was considered more serious than a shortage of Vitamin B. It was generally felt that you couldn't live without it. Grit, I've learned over the years, is one of the best things an old man has to offer a kid. That and fine lying, and maybe the proper use of the language.

Most of my early language training was attended to by old men. The first person to truly appreciate the value of this linguistic tutoring was my Freshman Composition teacher in college. He called me into his office and told me that my composition papers were filled with the most outrageous lies ever inflicted on the consciousness of a civilized and rational mind (meaning his) and that my spelling, grammar, and syntactical monstrosities approached the absolute in illiteracy. I was embarrassed. I just wasn't used to compliments like that. I thanked him, though, and said I realized I could write pretty good all right, but I reckoned I could do even better if I put my mind to it. Well, he was dumbfounded to hear that I might even surpass my previous literary efforts. As he gently shoved me out of his office, uttering over and over, "I don't *believe* it! I don't *believe* it!" I could tell he wasn't a man who knew anything about grit, or old men either.

For a long while when I was growing up, I didn't have an old man of my own, and had to borrow one belonging to a friend of mine. The old man was my friend's grandfather, which seemed to me like just about the most convenient arrangement a kid could ask for. Then my friend moved away and left the old man in his entirety to me alone. It was a fine stroke of luck. In the easy informality of the day, the old man called me "Bub" and I called him "Mr. Hooker." He didn't seem to mind the familiarity.

Mr. Hooker was a prime old man. One of the first things a kid learns about prime old men is that they don't put up with any kind of nonsense. Included in the vast store of things that Mr. Hooker considered nonsense were complaints, all of which he defined as "whining" or maybe on occasion "bawling like a calf." Consequently, when Mr. Hooker would take me out on cold winter days to check his trapline along Sand Creek, I would keep my complaints corked up until I could stand it no longer. Then I would articulate them in the form of a scientific hypothesis.

"I wonder what happens when a person's toes freeze plumb solid?" I would say.

"Wall, when they gets warm again, they jist thaws out," Mr. Hooker would reply, splattering a square yard of snow with tobacco juice. "Then they falls off."

I would respond to this news in a manner of appropriate indifference, as though I were unacquainted with anyone whose toes were at that moment in just such a predicament. Then Mr. Hooker would abruptly change the subject. "Say, Bub," he would ask me, "I ever show you how to build a fahr in the snow?"

"A couple of times," I would reply. "But I certainly wouldn't mind seeing it again."

Then Mr. Hooker would make a few magical motions with his feet and hands, and there would be a bare spot on the ground with a pile of sticks on it. He would snap the head of a kitchen match with his thumbnail, and before I knew what was happening we would be warming ourselves over a roaring fire, eating dried apricots, and talking of crows.

I couldn't begin to relate all the things I learned from Mr. Hooker, but maybe one will suffice. Even though he was in his late seventies and early eighties during the time that I knew him, he always insisted on climbing to the top of the mountain in back of our place to pick huckleberries. He taught me that the best huckleberries always grow on the top of the mountain. They weren't any bigger or sweeter or more plentiful up there than huckleberries growing at lower elevations. They were the best because they grew on top of the mountain. Some people may not understand that. If they don't, it's because they never had an old man to teach it to them.

The winter I was a senior in high school, Mr. Hooker almost died. It made him pretty damn mad, too, because he still had some things he wanted to do. I could imagine Death coming timidly into Mr. Hooker's hospital room and the old man giving him a tongue lashing. "You gol-durn ol' fool, you've come too soon! I ain't even used it all up yet!" He lived to greet another spring run of cutthroat trout up Sand Creek.

I was away at college the following winter when I got word that Mr. Hooker had at last used it all up. By the time I got home, the funeral was over and the relatives had come and gone, paying their last respects and dividing up among themselves his meager belongings.

"It would have been nice if they could have given you one of his fishing rods or a knife or something," my mother said. "I know he would liked to have left you something."

I decided to snowshoe out into the woods for a while, just to get away from people and hear what the crows had to say about the passing of Mr. Hooker. My eight-year-old nephew, Delbert, wanted to go along and try out his Christmas skis. Since I didn't consider him a people, I said, "All right, come on."

After we had tracked nearly the full length of the old trapline, Delbert raised an interesting point.

"What do you s'pose happens when a person's toes freeze plumb solid?" he said.

"Wall," I said, "they jist thaws out when they gets warm agin. Then they falls off. Say, Bub, I ever show you how to build a fahr in the snow?"

The Two-Wheeled ATV

My FIRST all-terrain vehicle was a one-wheel drive, and it could take you anywhere you had nerve and guts enough to peddle it.

Most of the other kids around had decent, well-mannered bicycles of distinct makes and models. Mine was a balloon-tired monster born out of wedlock halfway between the junkyard and the secondhand store. Some local fiend had built it with his own three hands and sold it to my mother for about the price of a good milk cow.

For two cents or even a used jawbreaker, I would have beaten it to death with a baseball bat, but I needed it for transportation. And transportation, then as now, was the name of the game.

You could walk to some good fishing holes, all right, but when the guys you were with all rode bikes, you had to walk pretty fast.

Perhaps the worst thing about the Bike, as I called it within hearing range of my mother, was that you simply could not ride it in a manner that allowed you to retain any sense of dignity let alone savoir-faire. The chief reason for this was that the seat was permanently adjusted for a person about six-foot-four. I was a person about five-foot-four. The proportions of the handlebars suggested strongly that they had been stolen from a tricycle belonging to a four-year-old midget. The result of this unhappy combination was that wherever I went on the Bike my rear was always about three inches higher than my shoulder blades.

I tried never to go any place on the Bike where girls from school might see me, since it was difficult if not impossible in that position to maintain the image I was cultivating among them of a dashing, carefree playboy.

The seat on the Bike was of the kind usually found on European racing bikes. The principle behind the design of this seat is that the rider goes to beat hell the sooner to get off of it. The idea for heel-and-toe walking races was conceived by someone watching the users of these particular seats footing it back home after a race.

To get the proper effect of one of these seats, you might spend a couple of hours sitting balanced on the end of a baseball bat—the small end. Put a doily on it for cushioning.

Whatever the other guys thought of my appearance on the Bike, they had respect for me. I was the fastest thing around on two wheels, thanks to that seat.

The Bike had a couple of little tricks it did with its chain that the Marquis de Sade would have envied. One was that it would wait until you had just started down a long, steep, curving hill and then reach up with its chain and wind your pant leg into the sprocket. This move was doubly ingenious, since the chain not only prevented you from putting on the coaster brakes, it also shackled you to a hurtling death-machine. Many was the time that a streamlined kid on a bike streaked silently past cars, trucks, and motorcycles on grades where a loose roller skate could break the sound barrier.

The Bike's other favorite trick was to throw the chain off when you needed it most. This usually happened when you were trying to outrun one of the timber wolves the neighbors kept for watchdogs. You would be standing up pedaling for all you were worth, leaving a trail of sweat and burned rubber two inches wide on the road behind you. The wolf would be a black snarl coming up fast to your rear. Then the chain would jump its sprocket and drop you with a crunch on the crossbar, the pedals still spinning furiously under your feet. The wolf gnawed on you until you got the chain back on the sprocket or until he got tired and went home.

The standard method for getting off the Bike was to spring clear and let it crash. If it got the chance, it would grab you by the pant leg at the moment of ejection and drag you along to grim destruction.

The Bike would sometimes go for weeks without the front wheel bouncing off. This was to lure you into a false sense of security. You would be rattling hellbent for home past the neighbors, and for a split second you would see the front wheel pulling away from you. Then the fork would hit the ground and whip you over the handlebars. Before you had your breath back, the wolf was standing on your belly reading the menu.

I spent half my waking moments repairing the Bike and the other half repairing myself. Until I was old enough to drive, I went around looking like a commercial for Band-Aids and mercurochrome. I hated to stop the Bike along the highway long enough to pick up an empty beer bottle for fear people would stop their cars and try to rush me to a doctor. Even on one of its good days, the Bike looked like an accident in which three people had been killed.

Much as I hated the Bike, I have to admit that it was one of the truly great all-terrain vehicles. It could navigate streams, cross fallen logs, smash through brush, follow a mountain trail, and in general do just about anything but climb trees. Several times it did try to climb trees but the damage to both of us was sufficient to make continued efforts in that direction seem impractical and unrewarding.

Our bicycles in those days were the chief mode of transportation for 90 percent of our camping trips. Occasionally even today I see people use bicycles for camping. They will be zipping along the road on ten-speed touring bikes, their ultralight camping gear a neat little package on the rear fender. When we went camping on our one-speed bikes, it looked as if we had a baby elephant on the handlebars and the mother on behind.

Loading a bicycle for a camping trip was not simply a remarkable feat of engineering, it was a blatant defiance of all the laws of physics. First of all, there may have been ultralight camping gear in those days, but we didn't own any of it. Our skillet alone weighed more than one of today's touring bikes, and a bedroll in cold weather, even without the feather bed, was the weight and size of a bale of straw. The tent was a tarp that worked winters as a haystack cover. A good portion of our food was carried in the quart jars our mothers had canned it in. Then there were all the axes, hatchets, saws, machetes, and World War II surplus bayonets without which no camping trip was complete. And, of course, I could never leave behind my jungle hammock, the pride of my life, just in case I happened to come across a jungle.

The standard packing procedure was to dump most of your stuff into the center of the tarp, roll the tarp up into a bundle, tie it together with half a mile of rope, and then find nine boys and a man to lift it to the back fender of the Bike. Anything left over was rolled up in the jungle hammock and tied to the diminutive handlebars. The hardware was distributed evenly around the outside of the two massive bundles, just in case you had sudden need for an ax or a bayonet.

Then you sprang onto the saddle and pedaled with all the fury you could generate from ninety-eight pounds of bone and muscle. The Bike would howl in rage, the twin humps of camp gear would shudder and sway like a sick camel, and slowly, almost imperceptibly, the whole catastrophe would move out of the yard and wobble off down the road on some incredible journey.

Sometimes during the winter now, when the cold awakens in my bones and flesh the ache of a thousand old injuries, I suddenly will recall in vivid detail the last few terrifying moments of the Bike's existence as a recognizable entity.

A ragged gypsy band of us had just begun another trip into the mountains on our camel-humped ATVs. As usual, I was far out in the lead, the hatchet-head bicycle seat urging me on.

There was a hill about three miles from my home called Sand Creek Hill, a name deceptive in its lack of color and description. By rights the hill should have been called Deadman's Drop or Say Goodby Hill. Loggers drove their trucks down it with one foot on the running board and one hand clutching a rosary—even the atheists.

Just as I crested the hill and started my descent, whom should I notice coming up it but one of our neighbors' wolves, apparently returning home after a hard night of killing elk in the mountains. From fifty yards away I could see his face brighten when he caught sight of me hurtling toward him like doom on two wheels. He crouched expectantly, his eyes happily agleam.

The chain, not to be outdone, chose that moment to eat my pant leg half way up to the knee. I expected to be abandoned by the front wheel any second. The washboard road rattled my bones; axes, saws, and bayonets filled the air on all sides; and the great straining mass of the rear pack threatened to collapse on me. With one last great effort, I aimed a quick kick at the wolf, ripped the pant leg free and threw myself into space. I bounced four times to distribute the injuries evenly about my body, and finally, using my nose for a brake, slid to a stop.

The Bike apparently self-destructed shortly after my departure. Probably the front wheel came off, and the two packs took it from there, ripping and tearing, mashing and grinding, until there was nothing left but a streak of assorted rubble stretching off down the hill.

Even the wolf was somewhat shaken by the impact of the crash. He stared at the wreckage in silent awe, almost forgetting my one good leg he held in his slack jaws.

When I was up and around once more, my mother bought me a car, my second ATV. She got it from a local fiend, who had built it with his own three hands, but that's another story.

The Backyard
Safari

CITY PLANNERS have shown beyond doubt that old orchards, meadows, and pine woods, which once threatened the outskirts of many of our towns and cities, can be successfully eradicated by constructing a housing development on top of them. To my knowledge there has not been a single recurrence of an old orchard, meadow, or pine woods after one application of a housing development.

Housing developments are a great boon to camping, since they make such fine places to get away from. At the same time, however, many of them are so designed that they are destroying one of the most exotic forms of camping known to man—the backyard safari.

The requirements for a backyard safari are few: a kid, a sleeping bag, and a backyard. The backyard is essential to the sport, and it saddens me that some developers have seen fit to phase it out.

I personally don't sleep out in the backyard much anymore. Oh, occasionally my wife will forget that I'm spending an evening out with the boys and, through some gross oversight, will remove the secret outside key from the geranium pot. An intimate association with slugs, night crawlers, and wandering dogs with terminal halitosis no longer holds the fascination for me it once did, and the ground has become much harder in recent years. Nevertheless there are those persons, mostly under the age of ten, for whom the backyard at night is still wilderness—a Mt. Everest, North Pole, and Amazon all rolled up in a seventy-five-foot-square patch of lilacs and crabgrass.

There are two distinct forms of Sleeping Out: With (Fred, John, etc.) and Alone. Both consist mainly of lying awake all night in the backyard. Otherwise they resemble each other about as much as hunting quail with a 12-gauge does shooting tigers with a blowgun.

At about age seven I gained easy mastery over Sleeping Out With, even though my first attempt was marred by a monumental miscalculation. We decided to sleep out in *his* backyard rather than mine. By daylight, the two backyards were separated by about a quarter mile of countryside laced with barbed-wire fences. At night, the distance was upwards of ten miles, laced with barbed-wire fences and populated by scores of creatures not yet known to science. It should be noted that in the aftermath of the harrowing experience of that first night I could remember distinctly the features of several weird, hairy creatures that flitted past but could not recollect having passed through, over, or under a single barbed-wire fence.

Vern, my camping buddy, and I had snuggled down into our foot-high pile of quilts, comic books, and assorted edibles and were well on our way to spending a pleasantly adventurous night under the stars. Then it got dark. Sometime between 9 P.M. and midnight, I became convinced that the forces of darkness were conspiring to terminate my existence. I emerged from beneath the quilts and prepared to hurl my body out into the abyss of night, informing Vern that I had suddenly recalled some urgent business at home that cried out for my immediate attention. He took the news badly, since he had no experience in Sleeping Out Alone and had no intention of gaining any until he was about forty-seven. His argument for my staying was fierce and brilliant, but it couldn't hold a candle to the pure, hard logic of a wavering screech which at that moment drifted out of the nearby woods. Neighbors said later that they noticed a terrible smell of burned rubber hanging on the air next day, but I think they were exaggerating. Melting the soles off a pair of tennis shoes just doesn't smell that bad.

Sleeping Out With allows for a certain degree of sloppiness and haphazard good fellowship, but Alone is all serious business, fraught with craft, skill, and ritual. Some great writers have suggested that initiation into manhood has something to do with getting your first gun, deer, bear, drink of whiskey, or some other such first, but they are wrong. The true initiation into manhood consists of Sleeping Out Alone in your backyard for the very first time. You can almost always recognize a kid who has just completed this ritual. There will be a slight swagger to his gait, and a new firmness to his jaw —and he will be old and wrinkled and have white hair.

The first step in Sleeping Out Alone is to select just the right spot on which to spend the night. If it is too close to the house you will draw such taunts as, "Albert is spending the night on the back stoop." On the other hand, the sleeping spot should not be so far from the house that the distance cannot be covered in less than two seconds starting from a prone position.

An imaginary straight line extends from the sleeping spot to the back door of the house. This line should be cleared of all obstacles: hoses, lawn chairs, tall blades of grass. If one has a dog, he should be tied or locked up well before night in order to prevent his slipping in under cover of darkness and surreptitiously depositing a new obstacle on the escape route. Dogs have also been known to fall asleep directly on the beeline, as it is sometimes called. Once while traveling at a high rate of speed, I collided with my old dog, Strange, under just such circumstances. The result was multiple bites on the legs, neck, head, and hindquarters, but after a good deal of rest and medication he managed to pull through.

Choice of sleeping gear is largely a matter of preference. Most youngsters prefer to sleep with all their clothes on, although some find it more comfortable to wear only their underwear and shoes. Blankets on an old mattress have the advantage over sleeping bags of being easier to eject from in an emergency. Mummy-type sleeping bags should be avoided, since a stuck zipper may force one to run completely encased in the bag. While by no means impossible, running under such a handicap will cut one's speed nearly in half. Another hazard is that mothers have been known to faint and fathers to screech out strange obscenities at the sight of a mummy bag suddenly bounding into the house.

On a youngster's first attempt at Sleeping Out Alone, the considerate family usually waits up and throws him a little welcoming party shortly before midnight. If the sleeper-out is unprepared for such a reception, he will probably enter the kitchen fully accelerated and wearing the expression of a person possessed of the knowledge that he is being closely pursued by something large and hairy. Under these circumstances it is best if the parents avoid leaping out of hiding places and yelling "Surprise!" The youngster will probably recover from the shock but the kitchen may not. In any case the parents will be creating some distasteful and unnecessary work for themselves.

The eight-year-old who takes it upon himself to sleep alone in the backyard, nine times out of ten, harbors in his heart some hope of one day becoming a mountain man or maybe a cowboy. Everyone knows that the ability to sleep outside alone is a prerequisite for both professions. Also one may wish to squelch once and for all the suspicion among his peers and siblings that he is "chicken." There is nothing that so assaults a man's self-respect as to have an older sister spread the rumor around the neighborhood that her little brother has a gizzard. Thus the sleeper-out who suddenly decides that the better part of valor is to get the hell inside the house as quickly as possible may want to assume some sort of protective coloration, if for no other reason than to hide his ruffled feathers.

The wise youngster, therefore, will decelerate abruptly at the back door, compose himself, and enter his abode with a bearing that exudes dignity, calmness, and self-assurance. He must then be prepared to undergo a certain amount of friendly but mischievous interrogation concerning the reasons for his premature return. Should he be so unsophisticated as to give his actual reasons, he is likely to receive some such response as, "Well, that's strange. I don't recall ever seeing a grizzly bear in the backyard before. A few mountain lion tracks among the azaleas maybe, but no grizzly bear."

Consequently, it is best to have a few plausible answers worked out well in advance, such as, "I thought

I smelled smoke and rushed in to wake the family," or, "I nearly forgot, but I'm expecting an important phone call this evening."

The night that I Slept Out Alone successfully for the first time was probably typical for such undertakings, except it was rather long—about equal in length to the time required for the rise and fall of the Roman Empire. The only part of me that slept at all that night was my right hand, and that only because it was wrapped so tightly around a baseball bat. Several times, off in the distance, an ant coughed. The night dragged on. A pack of wolves circled my camp. Darkness embraced the earth. An ax murderer passed through the yard on his way to work. Where *is* the sun? I thought. It *must* be nearly dawn. A siren sounded faintly in a distant town. The ten o'clock curfew. I had been Sleeping Out Alone for forty-five minutes. I sniffed the air for smoke, hoping that the house might be burning down, and I could rush in and save the family. I was expecting an important telephone call, but we had no phone. Inside the house, I knew my sister, The Troll, lay awake listening for the thunder of my footsteps on the porch. She was sorting and polishing her hoard of "chicken" phrases. I slouched back down into the saddle of my self and grimly rode against the night.

Shooting the Chick-a-nout Narrows

MY LOVE OF RAFTING started in grade school and lasted up until I was thirty years old, or, to be more exact, until about fifteen seconds before my buddy Retch and I became the first persons to shoot the Chick-a-nout Narrows and live.

A teacher by the name of Miss Goosehart got me started on rafting. I was about ten at the time with an academic record that would make a turnip look like an overachiever. One day Miss Goosehart kept me after school and told me she was going to make me literate if it killed her. I said all right I'd do it if she promised not to tell my mother. What she wanted me to litter I had no idea, but I was too smart to let on. Miss Goosehart, her eyes filling with tears, apparently gave up on the idea of forcing me into a life of crime, and instead thrust a book into my hands. "Here," she said. "Read this as soon as you learn how."

The book had pictures in it of this kid and a man floating a raft down a river. They had a little tent pitched on the raft, and a fishing line trailing behind in the water. You could tell from looking at their faces that the two of them were having themselves a fine time. I sounded out their names. H-u-c-k and J-i-m. Pretty soon I was overwhelmed by curiosity and started sounding out the first sentence in the book. I sounded faster and faster. By the time I had sounded out the first chapter I knew how to read. Ol' Miss Goosehart had hooked me on reading. It was a terrible thing to do to an innocent kid who wanted nothing more out of life than to fish and hunt and maybe run a trapline in the off season.

By the time I had finished reading *The Adventures of Huckleberry Finn*, I already had a raft of my own built. A kid by the name of Harold helped me build it, but I was the brains behind the project. Since there weren't many logs to be found lying along the banks of Sand Creek, we used old cedar fenceposts. We tied the fenceposts into bundles with rope and baling wire, and then lashed the bundles of fenceposts to a couple of rotten planks. The raft was by no means as attractive as it might appear from this description, but I had little doubt that it would serve the purpose. The little doubt I did have moved me to offer some words of advice to Harold, particularly since Sand Creek was at flood stage and doing its best to wash out roads, bridges, pump-houses, and anything else that might offer it some amusement.

"I bet this raft would hold ten people," I told Harold proudly.

"I bet it would hold twenty people," Harold said.

"You're probably right," I said. "But when we test it, I think only one of us should be on it."

"Good idea," Harold said.

"And," I said, "I think it would be best if you

stand right in the center of the raft so you don't fall overboard when I shove it out into the current."

"I bet it might not even hold one person," Harold said. "And I'm wearing my good pants. You go."

Harold may not have been a great naval architect, but he wasn't dumb. Why hadn't I thought to wear my good pair of pants!

There was nothing to do but make the test float myself. Gingerly I climbed aboard, making a mental note that the raft bobbed about a good deal and that the posts seemed to be spreading apart under my weight. These were not good signs, particularly since the raft was not yet in the water.

Nevertheless, I decided to have a short float. Harold and I first tried christening the raft with a bottle of orange pop, but the bottle refused to break. Since there was every indication we might pound the raft apart before it did so, we drank the pop instead. Then I hopped aboard. Harold pushed the raft out into midcurrent and I was on my way. From that moment on, Harold did not refer to his pants as his good pants. He called them his lucky pants.

"How far you going?" Harold shouted.

"Not far," I yelled back. "Just a mile or two."

I must say that I have enjoyed few things in life as much as I did the first ten seconds of my ride on that raft. Then I perceived that the fenceposts were sinking under my feet. Not sinking fast, mind you, but rapidly enough to hold my interest. By the time I rounded the first bend, the raft was completely beneath the surface and the water was lapping at my ankles. Fortunately the raft stabilized at that point, and I continued drifting precariously along, my attention more or less equally divided between retaining some degree of dignity and looking for the first opportunity to disembark.

The spectacle of my apparently standing on the

surface of Sand Creek was not without its rewards. It stimulated a herd of milk cows to race wildly about their pasture in an amusing fashion, sent several dogs slinking for home with their tails between their legs, and brought the Petersons' hired hand to his knees, whether out of laughter, shock, or just reverence I never found out.

Gossips later reported to my mother that I had been seen walking on water and, from observations of the final stage of my journey, floating down Sand Creek with a bundle of fenceposts under each arm. Ol' Mom was furious. She told the gossips I got in enough trouble without folks making up lies about me.

Over the years I built up a couple dozen rafts, all of them vastly superior to that initial effort. My first rafting experience, however, taught me numerous lessons about naval architecture, the most important of which is that when the time comes for the test float to make sure that you are the only one of the crew wearing his good pants. In fact, I have noticed that even when a cost-plus aircraft carrier is launched the people responsible for it are standing around in the best clothes money can buy, and the reason is they started out their careers building fencepost rafts.

Eventually I grew up, a fact that surprised many of our neighbors, some of whom lost good money betting against that likelihood. One of the problems of being a grownup was that I no longer had the time to build log rafts. It occurred to me one day that the next best thing would be a rubber raft. My search for such a raft led me ultimately back to my hometown and to an establishment I had frequented much as a kid—Grogan's War Surplus.

When I emerged from the tunnel of jerrycans, ammo boxes, and landing nets that formed the entrance to the store, Henry P. Grogan, the proprietor, was hunched over a counter pasting little paper swastikas on some battered GI mess kits. I was glad to see he hadn't changed over the years, and was reminded of the long-standing business arrangement we had worked out between ourselves when I had frequented his store as a kid: Grogan would try to sell me every worthless, rotten, rusty piece of junk he couldn't peddle to anyone else. I would buy it. The arrangement seemed equitable enough at the time, and both of us were satisfied with it. Now, of course, I was no longer a kid still wet behind the ears. I chuckled to myself at the thought the old codger might even now try to pull a fast one on me.

When he saw his former associate, Grogan's face erupted into a snaggletoothed grin. He swooped down upon me like a chicken hawk on a Rhode Island red.

"How's business, Mr. Grogan?" I asked after he had extracted from me the history of my life since leaving home.

"Not so good," he said, shaking his head. "It dropped off sharply about the time you went to college. Which reminds me, I'm running a special on some fine parachute harnesses if you're interested."

"Afraid not," I said.

"How about a gen-u-wine antique Nazi mess kit, then? Just happened to come across one in the cellar."

"No," I said. "I still have a dozen left over from the old days. What I am looking for is a surplus seven-man rubber life raft."

Grogan's face clouded over. "Hell, boy, I ain't had one of them in a couple of years."

"What!" I shouted in dismay. "You don't have one?" It was as if a door had slammed shut on an era, and I hadn't heard it. Never in my life had I gone to

Grogan with money in my pocket that he didn't have what I wanted.

"I don't rightly know where you could find one of them rafts anymore," Grogan said, scratching his head as though he too was confused by it all. "Maybe you could find a brand-new raft in one of the sporting-goods stores."

"No," I said. "I've priced them and they're too expensive. All I've managed to save up for a raft is fifty dollars. Well, it sure has been good talking to you again anyway, Mr. Grogan."

"Fif . . . fif . . ." Grogan said, as if about to sneeze. "Ah, hold on there a minute, son, let me ponder this a spell." Then his face split into that old ambergris grin that once had shown down regularly upon my head like the sun at high noon. He scurried out a back door and shortly returned, dragging behind him a greasy yellow amorphous mass.

"What's that?" I asked.

Grogan wiped his hands on his shirt. "This, my boy, is a gen-u-wine seven-man war-surplus rubber life raft I'd forgot. I spread it out over some old jeep trans-missions in the yard a while back to weather a bit. Rubber life rafts like lots of sun and water, ya know. Don't know what suddenly made me remember it."

"That doesn't look to me like it would hold seven men," I said.

"The way the War Department figured these things," Grogan said, "was two men in the raft rowing and five men in the water holdin' on for dear life. That's why they calls it a life raft."

Well, I was absolutely delighted. "How much?"

"Fifty dollars."

I was so elated at having found a raft that I had it home and half inflated before it occurred to me to feel behind my ears. Sure enough, definite signs of moisture.

What Grogan had sold me was not your ordinary seven-man rubber life raft. No. Although I couldn't be certain I was reasonably sure this was the very same raft I had once seen in one of those World War II movies set in the South Pacific. It was the one where the bomber crew has had to ditch in the ocean, and the pilot suddenly yells, "Dang it all to heck, men, the last burst from that Zero riddled our life raft!"

I yelled, too, all the time I was patching up the raft, a task just slightly more complicated than performing abdominal surgery on a hippopotamus. My yells, however, registered a good deal higher than the pilot's on the scale of profanity, and called into question the ancestry of the raft, the War Department, the Zero, and last but not least, Henry P. Grogan.

By the time the raft was finally repaired it looked like some creature from the lower depths that had died of yellow jaundice, bloated and popped to the surface where it had advanced into one of the later stages of decay. Like my first raft, it was not an attractive vessel.

My friend Retch and I would inflate the raft at home with the blower on my wife's vacuum cleaner and then tie it to the top of Retch's small foreign car to haul to a river. Once we were stopped by two highway patrolmen. One of them said he had thought the reason Retch was exceeding the speed limit in a restricted zone was that we were trying to get away from a giant slug that had grabbed our car. I must say it gives the police a bad image when two officers giggle hysterically while one of them is writing you out a ticket.

The raft rekindled in me my old addiction for floating down creeks and rivers. Every spare minute that we could get away from our jobs, Retch and I were either floating down a river or poring over maps to find a good river to float down. We floated streams just deep enough to be called damp. On the other extreme, we floated the Snake and Columbia, both of which had stretches of water that could make a man drunk with fear just looking at photographs of them. Retch and I shot rapids that made our hair stand on end so hard the follicles turned inside out. Sometimes we had to bail the cold sweat out of the raft to keep from swamping. And we called it a whole lot of fun.

"M-m-man," we would say to each other, "that was f-f-fun!"

As we grew older—sometimes on the raft we would age a couple of years in just five seconds—we began to prefer relaxing floats down gentle rivers, maybe catching a few fish or spending a couple of days hunting in a remote area. Once in a while we would be surprised to find ourselves bouncing along over what we called "interesting water," but for the most part these floats were without excitement.

One hunting season Retch and I were going over our maps when we found this river that wound through a thirty-mile stretch of uninhabited country. It looked like just the place for a combined float and deer-hunting trip. On the map the river appeared calm enough, but we decided to ask around and see if we could find someone who had floated it. We talked to several people who said they'd been down the river and they told us about the only thing we had to worry about was that the river would be deep enough to float the raft.

"But watch out for the Narrows," they all said, almost as an afterthought. Then they would describe the horrors of the Narrows, how the river squeezed be-tween these two rock walls, at the same time dropping

over a series of waterfalls and making several right angle
turns, boiling over rocks the size of houses standing on
end, and . . .

"Enough!" we said. "Just tell us where the
Narrows are located."

No one seemed exactly sure about their location.
"You can't miss 'em, though," one fellow said. "You'll
know 'em when you see 'em."

That was what threw us off.

On the first day of the float, Retch and I left our
car at the lower end of the river and hired a local
rancher to haul us, Retch's dog Smarts, and our raft
and gear up to the jumping-off place. You would have
thought the rancher had never been confined in a
pickup with two madmen before, he was so nervous.

"What for you fellas wanta float that doughnut
down the river?" he asked.

"Wanta do some deer hunting," I said.

"Hell," he said. "You could hunt deer on my
ranch. Be glad to get rid of a couple of them. Critters
are eatin' me right into the poor house."

"Naw," Retch said, "Huntin' that way is too
easy. We like to make it as hard as possible."

The rancher didn't say much after that, no
doubt fearing for his life. Anyone crazy enough to float a
doughnut down a river just to make deer hunting hard
might grab you by the throat if you happened to say the
wrong thing. After we had unloaded on the bank of the
river, he rolled his window down just enough so that a
madman couldn't lunge through and grab a person by
the throat. "Watch out for the Narrows," he yelled, and
then tore off up the road.

Our first day on the river was pleasant enough,
almost without incident. Then toward evening Smarts,
who had been asleep on the pile of rubberized duffle
bags, leaped to his feet and sounded a warning.

Shortly, we too could hear the ominous roar of water off in the distance.

"The Narrows!" I said. "We'd better go ashore and have a look at them."

Well, we had to laugh at the way folks tend to exaggerate. The river did squeeze into a narrow channel between these two big rocks all right, then tumble down a stair-step fall and finally break into a rather modest rapid. "Har, har, har!" we laughed. "So that's the infamous Narrows! Har, har, har!" The only water we took in the raft was tears from laughing so hard.

"Imagine," Retch said, wiping his eyes. "Grown men chickening out from shooting the Narrows!"

"I hereby name them the Chick-a-nout Narrows," I yelled, waving my paddle over the river like a scepter. "The Chick-a-nout Narrows!"

From then on we relaxed and just enjoyed ourselves, our former anxiety over the Chick-a-nout Narrows now merely a source of amusement. We laughed every time one of us mentioned them. "Har, har, har!"

We spent the next day hunting, without success. We started out with the idea of shooting a couple of trophy bucks and finally settled for the possibility of bagging a couple of hamburgers at a drive-in on our way home. When we staggered exhausted into camp that evening, Retch said, "Hey, what's say we throw our gear on the raft and float out of here tonight? After all we don't have to worry about the Chick-a-nout Narrows anymore. Har, har, har!"

"Good idea," I said "Har, har, har!"

As the raft bobbed gently along on the moonlit river, we would take turns dozing. Sometimes we would forget who was supposed to be dozing and we would both doze. On one of these occasions, I awoke with a start and noticed that the momentum of the river had picked up considerably. Also the river was deeper. The reason the river was deeper was that it was flowing through a channel between two sheer rock walls, and the channel was getting—I hate to think of the word—*narrow!*

"Hey, the river is getting narrow!" I yelled.

"Har . . . ?" Retch said, popping up in the raft.

Smarts whimpered. His hair stood out like the quills of a porcupine under attack.

Up ahead the rock walls came together to form a narrow black crack. Occasionally a big glob of foam would spout up into the crack, sparkle for a moment in the moonlight, then drop back into the darkness. Retch and the dog and I all shouted directions to each other but all we could hear was the sound of thunder emanating from the black crack. The three of us churned the river into a froth trying to paddle back upstream. And then the current sucked us into the Narrows.

I will not attempt to tell what shooting the Narrows in the middle of the night was like—about the paddles snapping in our hands like match sticks, about the river wrapping the raft around us like dough around three frightened wieners, the drop-offs, the drop-ups, the part where we were walking horizontally around the walls carrying the raft, the part where the raft was on top of us and the river was on top of the raft, and certainly not about the parts where it got bad. It will suffice to say that when we finally emerged from the Narrows, I was paddling with a boltaction .30-06, Retch was paddling with the dog, and there was no sign to be found of the raft.

Only in recent years has some of the old yearning for rafting returned, but I have no trouble fighting it off. Retch doesn't care much for rafting anymore either, but he has at last reached the point where he can joke about the Chick-a-nout Narrows. He lets on as if he still can't stand the sound of rushing water. If someone turns on a faucet too near him, he pretends to go all white in the face and starts shouting, "Watch out for the Narrows! Watch out for the Narrows!"

The Miracle of the Fish Plate

WHEN I WAS A KID, my family belonged to the landed aristocracy of nothern Idaho: we owned the wall we had our backs to. We were forced to the wall so often that my mother decided she might as well buy the thing to have it handy and not all the time have to be borrowing one.

Part of our standard fare in those days was something my grandmother called gruel, as in "Shut up and eat your gruel!" My theory is that if you called filet mignon "gruel" you couldn't get most people to touch it with a ten-foot pole. They would rather eat the pole. But when you call gruel "gruel," you have a dish that makes starvation look like the easy way out.

My mother shared this opinion. She preferred to call gruel "baked ham" or "roast beef" or "waffles," as in "Shut up and eat your waffles." One Christmas when we were hunched against the wall, she had the idea of thickening the gruel, carving it, and calling it "turkey." We were saved from this culinary aberration by a pheasant that blithely crashed through one of our windows to provide us with one of the finest Christmas dinners it has ever been my pleasure to partake of—*pheasant et gruel.* Mom said that God had sent us the pheasant. I figured that if He hadn't actually sent it, He had at least done His best by cursing the pheasant with poor eyesight and a bad sense of direction.

In that time and place, wild game was often looked upon as a sort of divine gift, not just by us but by many of the poor people, too. Hunting and fishing were a happy blend of sport, religion, and economics, and as a result, game was treated with both respect and reverence. In recent years, my affluence has increased to the point where I can dine out at Taco Tim's or Burger Betty's just about anytime I please, so I must admit that hunting and fishing are no longer economic necessities to me. To the contrary, they are largely the reasons I can't afford to dine out at better places, Smilin' John's Smorgasbord, for example. I still regard the pursuit of game as primarily a mystical, even religious quest. To tie into a lunker trout is to enter into communion with a different dimension, a spiritual realm, something wild and unknown and mysterious. This theory of mine was comfirmed by no less an authority than a Catholic priest with whom I occasionally share fishing water.

"Me lad," he said, "whenever yourself catches any fish a-tall 'tis a miracle."

I personally would not go so far as to say that my catching a fish would fall into the category of miracles . . . except . . . well, yes, there was one time. You might call it The Miracle of the Fish Plate.

When I was nine years old and the only angler in our family, my catching a fish was a matter of considerable rejoicing on the part of not only myself but my mother, sister, and grandmother as well. There was none of that false praise one occasionally sees heaped upon a kid nowadays—"Oh, my goodness, look at the great big fish Johnny caught! Aren't you just a little man!" No, there was none of that nonsense.

"Hey," my sister, The Troll, would yell. "P.F. Worthless caught a fish!"

"Looks like it's worth about three bites," my grandmother would say by way of appraisal. "But it's a dang sight better than nothin'."

"Put it on the fish plate," my mother would order. "Maybe by Sunday he will have caught enough so we can have fish instead of 'baked ham' for dinner."

The concept of the fish plate may require some explanation. My fishing was confined to a small creek that ran through the back of our place. In those far-off times, the legal limit was twenty-one trout. Although I had heard people speak of "limiting out," I never really believed them. It was an achievement beyond comprehension, like somebody running a four-minute mile, or walking on the moon. No one had ever fished with greater persistence and dedication than I, day in and day out, and I knew that it was not humanly possible to catch a limit of twenty-one fish. Six or seven maybe, but certainly not twenty-one!

Days would go by when I would not get even a single tiny nibble. I would send a hundred worms into watery oblivion for every solid bite. But every so often, suddenly, flashing in a silvery arc above my head, would be a caught trout, usually coming to rest suspended by line from a tree branch or flopping forty feet behind me in the brush. The notion of "playing" a fish seemed nearly as ridiculous to me as "limiting out."

Thus, one by one and two by two I would accumulate little six-, seven- and eight-inch trout over a period of several days (reluctantly releasing all fish less than six inches) until there were enough for a fish dinner. The collection place for these fish was a plate we kept for that purpose on the block of ice in the icebox. It was known as the fish plate.

I can say without any exaggeration whatsoever that our family watched the fish plate as intently as any investor ever watched a stock market ticker tape.

The summer of The Miracle of the Fish Plate was rather typical: we were living on gruel and greens; the garden was drying up for lack of rain; my mother was out of work; the wall had been mortgaged and the bank was threatening to foreclose. But good fortune can't last forever, and we soon fell on hard times. It was then that we received a letter from a wealthy relative by the name of Cousin Edna, informing us that she would be traveling in our part of the country and planned to spend a day visiting with us. That letter struck like a bolt of lightning.

The big question was, "What shall we feed Cousin Edna?" Cousin Edna was a cultured person, a lady who in her whole life had never once sat vis-à-vis a bowl of gruel. Certainly, we would not want her to get the impression we were impoverished. After all, we had a reputation to maintain befitting the landed aristocracy of northern Idaho.

After long deliberation, my mother fastened a hard cold eye on me, which I can tell you is just about as disgusting as it sounds. "All we can do is have fish for dinner," she said. "How's the fish plate?"

"It's got two six-inchers on it," I said.

"Pooh!" my grandmother said. "There's no way he's gonna catch enough trout before Cousin Edna gets here. The boy's just slow. And he's got no patience and is just too damn noisy to catch fish. Why his grandfather used to go to the crick and be back in an hour with a bucketful of the nicest trout you could have ever laid eyes on."

As you may have guessed, my grandfather was not one of the country's great conservationists. Although he died before my time, his ghost hovered about, needling me about my angling skills. My grandmother attributed his great fishing success to his patience and silence. Personally, I figured he probably used half a stick of dynamite as a lure.

"Don't tell me we have to depend on P.F. Worthless!" my sister wailed. "We'll be humiliated!"

"I'll catch all the fish we need," I yelled.

"Shut up," Mom said, soothingly. "If worse comes to worst, we'll let Cousin Edna eat the two fish we have and the rest of us will pretend we prefer 'baked ham.'"

"It ain't gonna wash," Gram said. "The best we can hope for is another deranged pheasant."

The gauntlet had been hurled in my face. It was up to me to save the family pride, or die trying.

I dug my worms with special care, selecting only those that showed qualities of endurance, courage, and a willingness to sacrifice themselves to a great cause. By that time of year, I had fished the creek so thoroughly that I had cataloged almost every fish in it, knew them all on a first name basis, and was familiar with their every whim and preference. They, on the other hand, knew all my tricks. It would not be easy enticing them to take a hook but I was determined to do it.

And it was not easy. I knew where a nice eight-inch brookie was holed up under a sunken stump. In the grim cold light of first dawn, when he would not be expecting me, I crawled through the wet brush and stinging nettles just above his hideout. I waited, soaked, teeth chattering quietly, passing the time by studying the waves of goosebumps rippling up and down my arms. As the first rays of morning sun began to descend through the pine trees, I lowered a superb worm, one blessed not only with dauntless courage but intellect as well, into the sluggish current that slid beneath the tangle of naked stump roots. I knew that I could not retrieve the hook without snagging it unless the point was covered by the mouth of a trout. Never was a finer bait presented so naturally, with such finesse. The line slackened, the hook drifting with the currents in the labyrinth of roots. A slight tremor came up the line. I whipped the rod back and the fat little eight-incher came flashing out from under the stump. He threw the hook and landed on the bank ten feet from me. I lunged for him, had him in my grasp. He slipped loose and landed in the water, where he circled frantically in an effort to get his bearings. I plunged in after him hoping to capitalize on his momentary confusion. Unfortunately, the water was much deeper than I expected and closed over my head like the clap of doom. As I dogpaddled my way into the shallows, I realized that filling the fish plate might be even more difficult than I had anticipated the chore would be.

Over the next two days I went up and down the creek like a purse seiner. My total take was two small fish, and Cousin Edna was arriving on the following day. I had become a nine-year-old existentialist, abandoning all faith and hope, driving myself on armed only with simple defiance of despair.

First the fish had abandoned me, then God, and now, on the final day, even the sun had slipped behind the mountains, no doubt sniggering to itself. Before me lay the bleakest, shallowest, most sterile part of the creek. Never in my whole life had I caught a fish there, mostly because it would have been pointless to even try. The water rippled over a bed of white gravel without a single place of concealment for even the smallest trout. Well, possibly there was one place. A small log was buried in the gravel diagonally to the current, and I noticed that at the downstream tip of the log there appeared to be a slight pooling of water. I eased into the stream and crept up to the butt end of the log, whereupon I perceived that the gravel had been washed from under it to form a narrow trough of dark, still water. I lowered my last worm, a pale, haggard, well-traveled fellow, into this trough and let it drift along the log, bumping over gravel, into limbs and knots, until it stopped. "Snagged!" I thought. Furious, I hauled back. My rod doubled over but the hook didn't come loose. Instead, the line began to cut a slow arc through the water, picked up speed, and then, exploding out onto the gravel bar, came what seemed to be a monstrous brook trout.

I cannot tell you how long the ensuing battle lasted because at my first glimpse of the fish, time ceased to exist, and the trout and I became a single pulsating spirit suspended in infinity. When at last we emerged into our separate identities, it was as victor and vanquished. In the dying light, the trout lay clamped between my aching knees on a white gravel beach, and I killed him with a sharp blow of a rock to the back of the head.

As he quivered into stillness, I was filled with unknown joy, unfamiliar sorrow. And I knew. I *knew*. Without the slightest doubt, I knew that under that same log, waiting in that watery darkness, was his twin.

Gently, I removed the hook from those great jaws, repairing the tatters of the heroic worm, threading them as best I could onto the hook, and made my way back to the log for a repeat performance. When you have a miracle going for you, you never want to waste any of it.

The dinner for Cousin Edna was a great success. When it was over and everyone had had his fill, there were still large sections of fried trout on the platter, which I suppose I need not tell you, was the humble fish plate.

"My heavens!" exclaimed Cousin Edna. "I just don't know when I've had a finer meal!"

"It's not over yet," said Gram. And then she served Cousin Edna a heaping bowl of wild strawberries that my sister had picked with her own little troll fingers.

The wild strawberries made Cousin Edna's eyes roll back in her head, they were so good. "Why, I hope you're not giving me all the strawberries," she said suddenly, noting our attentiveness.

"Land sakes," Gram said, "we have them so often we're tired of the little beggars." I looked at Gram in disbelief. It was the first time I'd ever heard her lie.

"We thought we would have some nice pudding instead," my mother said, passing around some bowls. I looked into mine.

"Hey," I said. "This looks like . . . this smells like . . ."

"Hush, dear," my mother said, her voice edged with granite. "And eat your *pudding*."

The
Backpacker

STRANGE, THE THINGS that suddenly become
fashionable. Take backpacking for instance.

I know people who five years ago had never
climbed anything higher than a tall barstool. Now you
can scarcely name a mountain within three hundred
miles they haven't hoofed up in their Swiss-made
waffle-stompers.

They used to complain about the price of sirloin
steak. Now they complain about the price of beef jerky
(which is about three times that of Maine lobster in
Idaho).

Their backpacking is a refined sport, noted for
lightness. The gear consists of such things as silk
packs, magnesium frames, dainty camp stoves. Their
sleeping bags are filled with the down of unborn goose,
their tents made of waterproof smoke. They carry two
little packets from which they can spread out a nine-

course meal. One packet contains the food and the other a freeze-dried French chef.

Well, it wasn't like that back in the old days, before backpacking became fashionable. These late-comers don't know what real backpacking was like.

The rule of thumb for the old backpacking was that the weight of your pack should equal the weight of yourself and the kitchen range combined. Just a casual glance at a full pack sitting on the floor could give you a double hernia and fuse four vertebrae. After carrying the pack all day, you had to remember to tie one leg to a tree before you dropped it. Otherwise, you would float off into space. The pack eliminated the need for any special kind of ground-gripping shoes, because your feet would sink a foot and a half into hard-packed earth, two inches into solid rock. Some of the new breed of backpackers occasionally wonder what caused a swath of fallen trees on the side of a mountain. That is where one of the old backpackers slipped off a trail with a full pack.

My packboard alone met the minimum weight requirement. It was a canvas and plywood model, sur-plus from the Second World War. These packboards ap-parently were designed with the idea that a number of them could be hooked together to make an emergency bridge for Sherman tanks. The first time you picked one up you thought maybe someone had forgotten to re-move his tank.

My sleeping bag looked like a rolled-up mat-tress salvaged from a fire in a skid row hotel. Its filling was sawdust, horsehair, and No. 6 bird shot. Some of to-day's backpackers tell me their sleeping bags are so light they scarcely know they're there. The only time I scarcely knew my sleeping bag was there was when I was in it at 2 A.M. on a cold night. It was freckled from one end to the other with spark holes, a result of my efforts to stay close enough to the fire to keep warm. The only time I was halfway comfortable was when it was ablaze. It was the only sleeping bag I ever heard of which you could climb into in the evening with scarcely a mark on you and wake up in the morning bruised from head to toe. That was because two or three times a night my companions would take it upon themselves to jump up and stomp out my sleeping-bag fires—in their haste neglecting to first evacuate the occupant. Since I was the camp cook, I never knew whether they were attempting to save me from immolation or getting in a few last licks for what they thought might be terminal indigestion.

Our provisions were not distinguished by variety. Dehydrated foods were considered effeminate. A man could ruin his reputation for life by getting caught on a pack trip with a dried apple. If you wanted apples, brother, you carried them with the water still in them. No one could afford such delicacies as commercial beef jerky. What you carried was a huge slab of bacon. It was so big that if the butcher had left on the legs, it could have walked behind you on a leash.

A typical meal consisted of fried bacon, potatoes and onions fried in bacon grease, a pan of beans heated in bacon grease, bacon grease gravy, some bread fried in bacon grease, and cowboy coffee (made by boiling an old cowboy in bacon grease). After meals, indigestion went through our camp like a sow grizzly with a toothache. During the night coyotes sat in nervous silence on surrounding hills and listened to the mournful wailing from our camp.

There were a few bad things, too, about backpacking in the old style, but I loved all of it. I probably would never have thought of quitting if it hadn't been for all those geophysical changes that took place in the Western Hemisphere a few years ago.

The first thing I noticed was a distinct hardening of the earth. This occurred wherever I happened to spread out my sleeping bag, so I knew that the condition was widespread. (Interestingly enough, my children, lacking their father's scientific training, were unable to detect the phenomenon.)

A short while later it became apparent to me that the nights in the mountains had become much colder than any I could remember in the past. The chill would sink its fangs into my bones in the pre-dawn hours and hang on like a terrier until the sun was high. I thought possibly that the drop in temperature was heralding a new ice age.

Well, I could put up with the hard and the cold but then the air started getting thinner. The only way you could get sufficient oxygen to lug a pack the size of an adolescent pachyderm was by gasping and wheezing. (Some of my wheezes were sufficient to strip small pine trees bare of their needles.) My trail speed became so slow it posed a dangerous threat to my person. If we were in fact at the onset of a new ice age, there was a good chance I might be overtaken and crushed by a glacier.

The final straw was the discovery that a trail I had traveled easily and often in my youth had undergone a remarkable transformation. In the intervening years since I had last hiked it, the damn thing had nearly doubled in length. I must admit that I was puzzled, since I didn't know that trails could stretch or grow. The fact that it now took me twice as long to hike it, however, simply did not allow for any other explanation. I asked a couple of older friends about it, and they said that they had seen the same thing happen. They said probably the earth shifted on its axis every once in a while and caused trails to stretch. I suggested that maybe that was also the cause for the ground getting harder, the nights colder, and the air thinner. They said that sounded like a plausible theory to them. (My wife had another theory, but it was so wild and far-fetched that I won't embarrass her by mentioning it here.)

Anyway, one day last fall while I was sitting at home fretting about the environment, a couple of friends telephoned and invited me along on a pack trip they were taking into the Cascades. Both of them are of the new school of backpacking, and I thought I owed it to them to go along. They could profit considerably by watching an old trail hand in action.

When I saw the packs R.B. and Charley showed up with I almost had to laugh. Neither pack was large enough to carry much more than a cheese sandwich. I carried more bicarbonate of soda than they had food. I didn't know what they planned to sleep in, but it certainly couldn't be in those tidy little tote bags they had perched on top of their packs. Anyway, I didn't say anything. I just smiled and got out my winch and they each got a pry pole and before you knew it we had my pack out of the car and on my shoulders. As we headed up the trail I knew it was going to be a rough trip. Already a few flakes of snow had fallen on my eyeballs.

The environment on that trip was even harsher than I had remembered. The trails were steeper, the air thinner, the ground harder, the nights colder. Even my trail speed was slower. Several porcupines shot past me like I was standing still.

R.B. and Charley showed obvious signs of relief when I made it into camp that first night.

"You probably thought I wouldn't make it with all the food," I chided them.

"No," R.B. said. "It was just that for a moment

there we didn't recognize you. We thought we were being attacked by a giant snail."

I explained to them that we old-time backpackers made a practice of traveling the last mile or so on our hands and knees in order to give our feet a rest.

It was disgusting to see them sitting there so relaxed and cheerful after a hard day's hike. They didn't seem to have any notion at all what backpacking was about. I could hardly stand it when they whipped out a little stove and boiled up some dried chunks of leather and sponge for supper. It probably would have hurt their feelings if I had got out the slab of bacon, so I didn't mention it. I just smiled and ate their food— four helpings in fact, just to make my act convincing. I never told them, but the Roast Baron of Beef was not quite rare enough for my taste and they had forgotten the cream sauce for the asparagus tips. And I have certainly tasted better Baked Alaska in my day, too.

Well, they can have their fashionable new-school backpacking if they want it. I'm sticking with the old way. Oh, I'm making a few concessions to a harsher environment, but that's all. When I got back from that trip, I did order a new pack frame. It was designed by nine aeronautical engineers, three metallurgists, and a witch doctor, and weighs slightly less than the down of a small thistle. My new sleeping bag weighs nine ounces, including the thermostatic controls. If I want to sleep in, my new cook kit gets up and puts on the coffee. Then I bought a few boxes of that dried leather and sponge. But that's all. I'm certainly not going to be swept along on the tides of fashion.

Great Outdoor
Gadgets
Nobody Ever
Invented

THOUSANDS OF ANGLERS no doubt consider the electronic fish-finder one of the top five achievements of the twentieth century, probably just behind the spinning reel and Einstein's theory of relativity. Personally, I feel the fish-finder is a nice enough gadget, but it is not high on my list of priorities for inventions needed to ease the lot of outdoorspersons. For some unknown reason, inventors specializing in hunting and fishing gadgets have never unleashed their ingenuity on the really tough problems plaguing men, women, and children who participate in outdoor sports.

After some thirty years of research on the subject, I now offer up to the inventors, without any hope or desire for recompense, my own list of inventions that nobody has yet invented.

There are any number of finders much more important than fish-finders, but I will mention only a couple of the more significant ones here.

Take the hunting-partner-finder, for instance. This would be used in situations where you have told your hunting partner, "I'll meet you at the top of that draw in an hour," and with malice aforethought, he immediately contrives to vanish from the face of the earth for the rest of the day. I have two ideas for this invention. One is simply a red balloon, attached to a quarter-mile length of string, that floats along above him. The other is a peanut-butter-seeking mechanical dog that will track him down and clamp a set of iron jaws on that portion of his anatomy adjacent to and slightly below the sack lunch he is carrying in his game pocket. Because you would merely have to stroll leisurely in the direction of the sound emanating from your hunting partner, this finder probably could be considered a sonar device.

Right at the top of my list of invention priorities is the mean-cow-finder. It would be used in this way. Say you want to fish a stream that winds through a cow pasture, which, as almost everyone knows, is the natural habitat of cows. A herd of the beasts will have taken up a good tactical position in the center of the pasture, enabling them to control all access routes to the stream and, more important, shut off the avenues of escape.

Now your average cow is a decent sort of animal, and I can put up with their mooing advice over my shoulder on how to improve my casting technique and choice of fly. I can even ignore their rather casual habits of personal hygiene, at least as long as they conduct their various indiscretions at a reasonable distance from where I am fishing. The problem is that it is almost impossible to distinguish a peace-loving cow from a mean cow, the kind who would swim Lake Erie to get a shot at you. What I have in mind is a simple little electronic gadget that would beep or flash a red light if a herd contained a mean cow. The more elaborate models might have a needle that would point out the malicious beast and maybe even indicate her aggression quotient and rate of acceleration from a standing start. I and a thousand anglers like me would trade in our fish-finders for a mean-cow-finder in a second, or sooner, I bet.

There are numerous gadgets and concoctions on the market for attracting game. What I need is something to repel game. Just last summer, for example, I could have made good use of a bear repellent. My wife and I were asleep in our tent in a remote area of Idaho when suddenly I awoke to the sound of the lid being ripped off our aluminum camp cooler.

"I think a bear just ripped the lid off our camp cooler," I hissed to my wife.

"I heard that," she replied sleepily. "I thought it was you in a hurry to find your pain-killer."

"Very funny," I said, hopping around in the dark in an effort to get my pants on. "Hand me the flashlight. I'm going out there and run the beggar off."

I unzipped the tent flap and switched on the flashlight. There in the beam stood a bear approximately the size of a boxcar; he was making a sandwich out of the camp cooler and appeared somewhat displeased at the interruption.

"HAAAAAYAAAAA!" I yelled. "GET OUTA THERE!"

"Did you run the beggar off?" my wife asked.

"I'M YELLING AT YOU! GET OUT OF THE TENT AND INTO THE CAR! I THINK WE'RE NEXT ON THE MENU!"

Not only would a little bear repellent have saved our camp cooler, it would have saved me the repeated tedium of having to listen to my wife regale my so-called friends with an account, including excessively exaggerated pantomime, of my reaction to the bear.

Inventors have made great strides on the problem of reducing the weight and bulk of backpacking equipment, but they haven't gone far enough. What I would like to see them come up with is a fully loaded backpack that is freeze-dried. When you had hiked into your campsite in the mountains you would merely have to take your backpack out of your pocket, soak it in a little water and, presto, you would have a reconstituted sleeping bag, tent, trail ax, cook kit and, of course, all your food.

When I told a backpacking friend about this idea, he scoffed at it. "Why not a freeze-dried log cabin with a flagstone fireplace?" he suggested, expanding on my concept.

'That's not bad," I told him.

Hell," he said, "you'd be the first one to complain about missing the weight of a good pack tugging at your shoulders, the soothing, rhythmical squeak-squeak of the frame and harness."

"For the past five years," I told him, "the rhythmical squeak-squeak of the frame and harness has been drowned out by the rhythmical squeak-squeak of my back."

I also have several suggestions for new sleeping-bag designs. One is primarily for use in small two-man tents. This consists primarily of a time-lock on the zipper so that once your tent partner is in his bag he can't get out of it until morning. My friend Retch spends most of the night crawling around, looking for one thing or another. This does not include his answers to nature's call. (On an average night Retch and nature conduct a regular litany between themselves.) Here is a typical verbal exchange he and I had in a tent recently:

"Watch out," I yelled at him. "You're kneeling on my glasses!"

"Sorry," he said. "I thought you still had them on."

"I do, you idiot!"

Another of my sleeping-bag inventions would be primarily for kids who are practicing "sleeping out" in the backyard. The bags would contain leg holes for running. This would save the kid the time required to strip off his sleeping bag in order to sprint for the house. These would be *valuable* seconds saved.

Speaking of children, I would like to see someone invent a small portable lie detector for use on kids while camping in remote wilderness campgrounds where the sole sanitary facility is a privy located at the far end of a quarter-mile trail intersected by logs, several small streams, and a skunk crossing, and frequently occupied with strange creatures that screech murderously at you in the dark. (Usually, these creatures are simply other parents you surprise hauling their tykes down the trail, but you never know.)

The lie detector would work like this: Just before their bedtime I would line the little ones up outside the tent and, one by one, attach them to the anti-fib device.

"Is your name Erin McManus?"

"Yes."

"Do you have a dog named Fergus?"

"Yes."

"Have you gone to the bathroom within the last fifteen minutes?"

"Yes."

"Hah! Hit the trail to the old privy, kiddo!"

Some kind of detector should be developed for the purpose of determining whether camp cooking is fatally poisonous. My own system, far from reliable, is to observe whether the *plat du jour* is killing flies and mosquitoes beyond a fifteen-foot radius. Some kind of chemically treated paper, on the order of litmus, would be perfect and a lot less expensive than seeing if the concoction will dissolve a spoon. I certainly could have used some of this poison detector a while back when Retch whipped up his infamous stew consisting of canned pork and beans, cabbage, beef jerky, and the miscellaneous leavings of a five-day hunting trip. Crammed into a tent with Retch and two other guys, I spent the night moaning in agony and praying for a quick end to it all. I don't know what would have happened to my present or future if I'd been dumb enough to eat any of the stew myself.

There are a number of life preservers for use by stream fishermen on the market now, but like so many other inventions designed for the outdoorsperson, their creators have stopped short of the mark. The basic idea of these life preservers is that if you fall in the water they can be inflated by blowing into a tube. With the kind of water I generally fall into, I don't want to waste any time blowing on some dumb tube. On some of the falls I've taken, I probably could have blown up a seven-man life raft before I hit the water if mere floating had been my chief concern. To hell with floating—what I need in the way of a life preserver is something that really preserves my life. As I see it, this would be a recording device installed in fishing vests. While I was contemplating whether to cross a peeled sapling over a sixty-foot-deep river gorge or possibly to make a running leap to land on a moss-covered rock in the middle of some rapids, the life preserver would activate automatically and shout through two stereo loudspeakers set at full volume, "DON'T TRY IT, YOU FOOL, DON'T TRY IT!"

The Purist

TWELVE-YEAR-OLDS are different from you and me, particularly when it comes to fishing, and most of all when it comes to fishing on Opening Day of Trout Season.

The twelve-year-old is probably the purest form of sports fisherman known to man. I don't know why. Perhaps it is because his passion for fishing is at that age undiluted by the multitude of other passions that accumulate over a greater number of years. Say thirteen.

Now I am reasonably sure that I can catch a limit of trout faster on Opening Day than the average twelve-year-old, but any angler knows that speed and quantity are not true measures of quality when it comes to fishing. It's a matter of style, and here the twelve-year-old beats me hands down. You just can't touch a twelve-year-old when it comes to style.

Preparation is the big part of his secret. If Opening Day of Trout Season is June 5, the twelve-year-old starts his preparation about the middle of March. He knows he should have started earlier, but at that age he likes to put things off. With such a late start, he will be hard pressed to be ready in time.

The first thing he does is to get his tackle out and look at it. He removes from one of his shoe boxes a large snarly ball of lines, hooks, leaders, spinners, flies, plugs, weeds, tree branches, and a petrified frog. He shakes the whole mass a couple of times and nothing comes loose. Pleased that everything is still in good order he stuffs it all back into his shoe box. The next time he will look at it will be on Opening Day Eve, fifteen minutes before he is supposed to go to bed. The tackle snarl will then provide the proper degree of wild, sweaty panic that is so much a part of the twelve-year-old's style.

The next order of business is to check his bait supplies. The best time to do this is in the middle of a blizzard, when it's too cold to be outside without a coat on or to have all the windows in the house open. The large jar of salmon eggs he has stored next to the hot water pipes that run through his closet seems to look all right, but just to be sure he takes the lid off He drops the lid on the floor and it rolls under something too large to move. Something must be done immediately, he knows, because uneasy murmurs are rising in distant parts of the house, and besides he won't be able to hold his breath forever. The best course of action seems to be to run the jar through every room in the building, leaving in his wake mass hysteria and the sound of windows being thrown open. Later, standing coatless with the rest of the family in the front yard while a chill north wind freshens up the house, he offers the opinion that he may need a new bottle of salmon eggs for Opening Day.

Occasionally the young angler will do some

work on his hooks. There is, however, some diversity of opinion among twelve-year-olds whether it is better to crack off the crust of last year's worms from the hooks or to leave it on as a little added attraction for the fish. The wise father usually withholds any advice on the subject but does suggest that if his offspring decides to sharpen his hooks on the elder's whetstone, the worm crusts be removed *before-hand*. Nothing gums up a whetstone worse than oiled worm dust.

The twelve-year-old takes extra-special pains in the preparation of his fly rod. He gets it out, looks at it, sights down it, rubs it with a cloth, sights down it again, rubs it some more, and finally puts it away with an air of utter frustration. There is, after all, not much that you can do to a glass rod.

The reel is something else again. A thousand different things can be done to a reel, all of which can be grouped under the general term "taking it apart." The main reason a kid takes his reel apart is to take it apart. But most adults can't understand this kind of reasoning, so the kid has to come up with some other excuse. He says he is taking his reel apart to clean it. No one can deny that the reel needs cleaning. It has enough sand and gravel in it to ballast a balloon. During most of the season it sounds like a miniature rock crusher and can fray the nerves of an adult fisherman at a hundred yards. For Opening Day, however, the reel must be clean.

There are three basic steps used by the twelve-year-old in cleaning a reel. First it is reduced to the largest possible number of parts. These are all carefully placed on a cookie sheet in the sequence of removal. The cookie sheet is then dropped on the floor. The rest of the time between March and the Opening Day of Trout Season is spent looking for these parts. The last one is found fifteen minutes before bedtime on Opening Day Eve.

Some twelve-year-olds like to test their leaders before risking them on actual fish. Nothing is more frustrating to a kid than having a leader snap just as he is heaving a nice fat trout back over his head. Consequently, he is concerned that any weakness in a leader be detected beforehand. There are many methods of doing this, but one of the best is to tie one end of the leader to a rafter in the garage and the other end to a concrete block. The concrete block is then dropped from the top of a stepladder. The chief drawback of this method is the cost involved in replacing cracked rafters.

Eventually the big night comes—Opening Day Eve.

The day is spent digging worms. Early in the season there is a surplus of worms and the young angler can be choosy. The process of worm selection is similar to that used in Spain for the selection of fighting bulls. Each worm is chosen for his size, courage, and fighting ability. One reason kids frequently have poor luck on Opening Day is that their worms can lick the average fish in a fair fight.

Approximately four hundred worms are considered an adequate number. These are placed in a container and covered with moist dirt. The container is then sealed and placed carefully back in the closet by the hotwater pipes, where it is next found during a blizzard the following March.

The twelve-year-old angler really peaks out, however, during that fifteen minutes before bedtime. He discovers that his tackle has become horribly snarled in his tackle box. No one knows how, unless perhaps the house has been invaded by poltergeists. The reel is thrown together with an expertise born of hysteria and panic. Four cogs, six screws, and a worm gear are left over, but the thing works. And it no longer makes that funny little clicking sound!

Finally, all is in readiness and the boy is congratulating himself on having had the good sense to start his preparation three months earlier. As it was, he went right down to the last minutes. Only one major task remains: the setting of the alarm clock.

Naturally, he wants to be standing ready beside his favorite fishing hole at the crack of dawn. The only trouble is he doesn't know just exactly when dawn cracks. He surmises about four o'clock. If it takes him an hour to hike down to the fishing hole, that means he should set the alarm for about three. On the other hand, it may take longer in the dark, so he settles on 2:30. He doesn't have to allow any time for getting dressed since he will sleep with his clothes on.

Once in bed he begins to worry. What if the alarm fails to go off? He decides to test it. The alarm makes a fine, loud clanging sound. After all the shouting dies down and his folks are back in bed, he winds up the alarm again. As a precautionary measure, he decides to set the alarm for two, thus giving himself a half-hour safety margin. He then stares at the ceiling for an hour, visions of five-pound trout dancing in his head. He shakes with anticipation. He worries. What if the alarm fails to awaken him? What if he shuts it off and goes back to sleep? The horror of it is too much to stand.

Midnight. He gets up, puts on his boots, grabs his rod and lunch and brand-new bottle of salmon eggs, and heads out the door.

It's Opening Day of Trout Season, and there's not a minute to spare.

The Outfit

YEARS AGO the Old Wilderness Outfitter started sending me his catalog of surplus outdoor gear: slightly battered canoes, scruffy rucksacks, dulled trail axes, tarnished cook kits, saggy tents, limp snowshoes, and the like. I spent many a fine winter hour thumbing through his catalog. Indeed, such was my enjoyment that occasionally I would lose control of my faculties and actually order some of the stuff. One surplus wilderness tent arrived with authentic wilderness dirt still on the floor, not to mention a few pine needles, a fir cone, a sprinkling of fish scales, and a really nice selection of squashed insects. The Old Wilderness Outfitter never charged for any of these extras, and in numerous other ways revealed himself to be a man of generosity and all-round good character. He put out a fine catalog, too.

The catalog arrived each winter with the same

regularity as the snow, and at about the same time. Then it stopped coming. I thought maybe the Old Wilderness Outfitter had died, or was peeved at me because I had sent a letter telling him I would just as soon furnish my own fish scales and squashed insects, and there was no need to include them with my orders. I hadn't intended to offend him though, and if sending the extras meant that much to him it was all right with me.

A few days ago, I was surprised to find in the mail a new catalog from the Old Wilderness Outfitter. Happily, I licked my thumb and started flipping through the pages. I was flabbergasted. There wasn't a single scruffy rucksack in the thing, let alone a slightly battered canoe. The Old Wilderness Outfitter had filled up his catalog with glossy, color pictures of beautiful people.

Glancing at the prices, I thought at first the beautiful people themselves must be for sale. There was one blonde lady who looked well worth the seventy-five dollars asked, and I would have been interested, too, if I didn't already have one of my own worth almost twice that amount.

Then I determined the prices were for the clothes the beautiful people were wearing! The seventy-five dollars wasn't the price of the blonde lady but what she had on, something described as "a shooting outfit." (I can tell you with absolute certainty that if that lady ever shot anything in her life it was a sultry look across a crowded room.) The men were almost as beautiful as the women, and dressed in a month's wages plus overtime. Their haircuts alone probably cost more than my shooting outfit, if you don't count my lucky sweatshirt with the faded Snoopy on it.

Most of the clothes were trimmed in leather

made from the hides of Spanish cows, which was appropriate, I thought, because most of the catalog copy was American bull.

After about ten minutes of studying the catalog, I could see what had happened. Some unemployed high-fashion clothes designers had got to the Old Wilderness Outfitter and persuaded him to chuck his rucksacks and the like and replace them with fancy clothes. The old codger should have known better. If American outdoorspersons were interested in fancy clothes, outdoor magazines would be written like this:

Doc stood up in the blind and squinted his eyes at the jagged rip of first light beyond the marsh. His closely woven virgin-wool shirt with the full sleeves and deep cape was beaded with rain.

"Hey, Mac," he said, "it's starting to rain. Better hand me my sage-green parka of water-repellent, super-tough eight-ounce cotton canvas duck with the hand-stitched leather flaps."

"Right," I said. "But first I'm going to drop that lone honker, which you'll notice is attractively attired in 100 percent goose down."

The truth is we outdoorspersons just aren't that interested in high fashion. Our preference runs more to low fashion. I myself have turned out a number of outstanding low-fashion designs. There was, for example, my free-form stain made by dropping an open bottle of dry-fly dressing in a shirt pocket. This design should not be confused with the one originating from a leaky peanut butter sandwich. My own favorite is the ripped pant leg laced shut with twenty-pound monofilament line, split-shot sinkers still attached.

Striking as these designs may be, I am just too

old to design really first-rate low fashions. I no longer have the time, patience, nerves, or stomach for it. As a matter of fact, low-fashion designers usually reach their peak about age fourteen. From then on they undergo a gradual decline until their last shred of self-respect is gone and they will think nothing of going out wearing, say (shudder) a brand-spanking-new red felt hat.

You'd never catch a fourteen-year-old wearing such a monstrosity as a new red felt hat. No sir. The first thing a fourteen-year-old does with a new hunting or fishing hat is to redesign it. Immediately upon returning home from the store, he turns the hat over to his dog. After the dog has exhausted his imagination and ingenuity on the hat, it is retrieved by the kid and pounded full of holes with a large spike and hammer. The edges of the holes are burnt with a match. This simulates the effect of the kid's having been fired upon at close range with an elephant gun. (Nobody knows why this is important to a kid, but it is.) A band of squirrel, skunk, or muskrat hide, more or less tanned by the kid himself, is fastened to the crown. Next the brim is folded up on three sides and pinned with the thigh bones of a fried chicken or other equally attractive fasteners. And finally, several tail feathers from a pheasant are artfully arranged about the crown. The hat now resembles the year-old remains of a high-speed collision between a large bird and a small mammal.

Not all youngsters, by the way, are born with this talent for low fashion. Some have to learn it. I recall an incident back in my junior high school days when my friends Retch and Peewee and I gave Hair Forsyth his first lesson in low fashion. (The nickname "Hair," by the way, derived from an observation by Retch, one of the more scholarly of my companions, that rich kids who stand to inherit the family fortune are known as "hairs.") Hair had taken to hanging out with us at school, and when it came time for the annual early spring camping trip, we thought we should invite him along. Several bare patches of earth had been reported to us, and we decided this was sufficient evidence that winter was over and camping weather had begun. There was still a bit of a chill in the air, not to mention several inches of snow on the ground, and we thought it likely that Hair would find these sufficient reasons for refusing our invitation. But he said he thought it was a great idea.

Since I lived out in the country at the edge of the Wilderness (sometimes referred to locally as Fergussen's woodlot and north pasture), our farm was selected as the jumping-off place for the weekend expedition. When Hair climbed out of his father's car that day, we regular low-fashion campers nearly burst trying to keep from laughing. Ol' Hair was dressed up just like a dude. He had on these insulated leather boots, special safari pants, a heavy wool shirt, a down jacket, a hat with fur earflaps, and so on. Naturally, we didn't want to hurt his feelings by pointing out how ridiculous he looked. Nevertheless, we thought we should instruct him on the proper attire for a spring camping trip.

"I hate to say this," Retch told Hair, "but you're absolutely gonna roast in all those clothes."

"Yeah," Peewee put in, "and those boots are gonna be awfully heavy for walking. Too bad you don't have tennis shoes like we're wearing."

"Right," I said. "Next time, Hair, why don't you see if you can get some tennis shoes like these, with holes in the canvas so the sweat can drain out."

Hair thanked us for straightening him out and said the next time he would have a better idea how to put together a suitable outfit.

After getting Hair squared away, we loaded up and headed out into the Wilderness. The snow out in the Wilderness was much deeper than any of us had expected. Bit by bit the depth of the snow increased until it was about halfway up to our knees. From time to time we would have to stop and chip the compacted snow off our tennis shoes and try to unplug the drain holes. These stops were occasion for much clowning around by us regulars for the benefit of Hair. Retch and Peewee would pound their feet against trees and make moaning and howling sounds, while I would tear off my tennis shoes and socks and blow on my blue feet in a comical manner. Hair laughed until tears streamed down his cheeks. Indeed, we all had tears streaming down our cheeks.

The wind came up shortly after it started to snow, and pretty soon we were slogging along through what we would have called a blizzard except that this was spring and the first of the good camping weather. Retch came up with the idea that maybe we should try to make it to an old abandoned trapper's cabin a couple of miles away and spend the night there.

"Otherwise, we might freeze to death," Retch joked.

"Heh," Peewee and I laughed.

"Freeze!" Hair cried. "You must be joking. I'm burning up inside of this darn coat. Dang, I hate to ask but, Peewee, could I get you to trade me your shirt for this coat? What do you call that kind of shirt anyway?"

"A t-t-t-t-t-tee shirt," Peewee said, thrusting it into Hair's hand.

"Well, I guess I'll just have to leave this wool shirt of mine behind unless I can get one of you fellas to wear it for me," Hair said, taking it off and putting on Peewee's T-shirt over his thick, creamy wool underwear.

I said, "Dang I'll wear it rather than have you leave it behind."

"That underwear's not too hot for you, is it?" asked Retch.

Hair said it wasn't, but that he sure wouldn't mind slipping his boiling feet into a nice cool pair of tennis shoes. So Retch says he has about the coolest pair of tennis shoes a person is likely to find, and he swaps shoes with Hair.

By dark we had made it to the trapper's cabin and had a roaring fire going in the barrel stove and **were** sitting around roasting ourselves a few marshmallows and listening to the wind howl outside. From then on, Hair was one of the regulars and, as far as I know, nobody ever again mentioned the ridiculous outfit he wore on that first camping trip with us. It was obvious to everyone that he had learned his lesson, and there was no point in hurting his feelings any more than was necessary.

The ultimate in low fashion, at least that I ever saw, was created spontaneously on one of our camping trips by Harold Munster, a tall, gangling, wild-haired youth whose chief claim to fame was an uncanny ability for taking a bad situation and making it worse. Sometimes you would be absolutely certain that a situation couldn't be any worse and then Munster would show up and make it nine times as bad as before.

Back in those days, our camping clothes were referred to by our mothers as "your OLD clothes." A mother would stick her head out the back door and yell at her kids, "Wear your OLD clothes, you hear!" Since all our clothes were old—most of them had been in our families longer than we had—OLD designated the old-est grade. OLD clothes were never discarded, they just faded away. Sometimes they faded away while you were wearing them, and that is what led to Harold Munster's creation of the ultimate in low fashion.

Retch, Peewee, Munster, and I had been back-packing for nearly a week and now were attempting to extricate ourselves from the mountains as expeditiously as possible. In part, this consisted in wild, free-for-all gallops down steep trails, with packs, axes, and iron skillets flailing about on all sides. It was during one of these maniacal charges downhill that Munster, hurtling a windfall, caught his OLD pants on a limb. The pants exploded in midair. Munster landed half naked in a shower of tiny bits of cloth, old patches, buttons, belt loops, and a broken zipper still held shut with a safety pin.

Well, we were all startled, a little embarrassed, and, of course, worried, because here was a bad situa-tion. Nobody knew in what manner Munster would strive to make it worse and which of us might be swept into the vortex of whatever catastrophe he came up with.

The mosquitoes in that area were about the size of piranhas and twice as voracious. As Hemingway might have put it, Munster had been turned into a move-able feast. His expanse of bare skin drew the mosquitoes off the rest of us like a magnet, and, though appreciative of the respite, we became concerned that our unfortu-nate companion might be eaten alive or, even more likely, slap himself to death.

A small spring issued from the edge of the trail at that point, creating a large muddy bog on the downhill side of the trail. Before we knew what was happening,

Munster had leaped into this bog and begun smearing his lower half with great globs of mud.

"Hey," he yelled up at us. "This really feels great!" We stared down at him with a mounting sense of foreboding, knowing from past experience that this was the beginning of something that would lead to dire consequences.

Not satisfied with coating his lower half with mud, Munster peeled off his OLD shirt and coated his upper half as well. Then he took handfuls of goop and rubbed it in his hair and on his face, all the while ooh-ing and ahhing with relief and saying, "This will take care of those blinkety-blank mosquitoes for a while."

The rest of us divided Munster's load up among ourselves so that his mud coating would not be rubbed off by his pack. Thus unburdened, he took the lead and strolled along light of heart and mosquito-free, occasionally whistling a few bars or counting cadence for the rest of us. As we plodded along and the day grew hotter, we noticed that Munster's mud coating was beginning to bake into a hard, whitish shell, with webs of tiny cracks spreading out from his joints and seams. Grass, moss, sticks, and small stones protruded from the shell in a rather ghastly manner. Munster began complaining about what he described as a blinkety-blank unbearable itch, and occasionally would stop wild-eyed and claw furiously at his mud cast. His claw marks served only to make his overall appearance even more grisly.

Our plan was to intersect a logging road and then try to catch a ride out of the mountains with some gyppo loggers who were working in the area. We encountered the loggers much sooner than expected. Three of them had hiked back in from the end of the road to eat their lunch by the edge of a small stream. They were now sprawled out resting, smoking, and digging the dirt out from among the calks on their boots. The trail we were on wound around the mountain about a hundred feet above them.

Retch, Peewee, and I had fallen some distance behind Munster, partly because of fatigue and partly because we could no longer endure the sight of him. As we rounded a bend in the trail, we caught sight of the three unsuspecting loggers, languid pools of tobacco smoke hanging in the still air about them. Poised like a silent gargoyle on the lip of the trail directly above this peaceful scene, was Munster, staring down at the loggers. We tried to shout but our tongues were momentarily paralyzed from the sheer horror of the scene before us. And then Peewee found his voice.

"MUNSTER!" he shrieked.

The startled loggers looked up. I could see the lips of one of them, puzzled, silently form the word "monster?"

Then Munster bounded down the hill toward the loggers, waving his arms ecstatically and croaking out his relief at being saved from having to walk the last ten miles home.

Walking the last ten miles home, we attempted to reconstruct the events of the ten seconds following Munster's lunge over the brink of the trail. It was agreed that we had all witnessed superb performances by three of the world's fastest gyppo loggers. Of particular interest was the fact that calked boots traveling at a high rate of speed throw up a fine spray of earth not unlike the plumes of water behind hydroplanes.

Harold Munster and his family moved away from town shortly after the last of his outfit wore off and I haven't seen him since, nor have I seen anything to match his masterpiece of low-fashion design. But if the Old Wilderness Outfitter had a lick of sense left, he would leave no stone unturned in his search for him.

Kid Camping

KIDS STILL DO GO CAMPING by themselves, I don't deny that. They just don't go *kid camping*.

A lot of people think that any camping kids do is kid camping just because kids are doing it. Well that's circular reasoning if I ever heard any. Nothing could be further from the truth. The kind of camping kids do nowadays is just plain adult camping—sans adults.

The kids use the same camp gear and provisions as their parents: featherweight sleeping bags, aluminum cook kits, nylon tents, dehydrated and vacuum-frozen foods, and even little plastic tubes to put their peanut butter and jelly in. The only exception is the family car, and *it* is used to haul the kids to the point of departure. They just don't get to drive.

Why it's enough to make an old-time kid camper roll over in his spaghetti-and-oatmeal omelet!

Properly executed, kid camping was like no other kind of camping known to man. I say "properly executed" because there was a code that governed every move. Any kid camper worth his can of pork 'n' beans knew the code by heart.

The code was not something that you learned, it was something you just *knew*—something you either had or you didn't have. And you never ever went against this thing that you knew. If you did, your camping was no longer kid camping but some other kind, and was divested of some peculiar aura of mystery and adventure.

Kid camping was a thing fairly choked in mystery. Part of the mystery was how a ninety-eight-pound boy who contracted an acute case of exhaustion carrying the dinner scraps out to the garbage pail could lug a four-hundred-pound pack three miles up a mountain trail laced with logs the size of railroad tank cars, and not even be winded. There was also the mystery of how three or four boys could consume every last moldering morsel of a food supply roughly estimated at a quarter ton and return home half starved.

One of the unspoken rules of the code (they were all unspoken) was that preparation for a camping trip should involve absolutely no planning. This, combined with an equal amount of organization, never failed to invest a trip with the proper mood—a deep and abiding sense of insecurity. There was a monumental apprehension that the food would give out an hour before the expedition arrived home and the whole party, fleeing back across the wasteland of the Crabtrees' stump pasture, would perish of starvation.

The only way of combating this dread of starvation was simply to carry enough food to feed Attila and his Huns adequately on an extended foray across Europe. It was assumed that each of the other guys would bring an equal amount.

The code allowed for only one store-bought item, the indispensable pork 'n' beans, which was the basic ingredient for all meals and most of the bad jokes. Wieners and marshmallows could also be purchased if the expedition was to be particularly arduous. These were generally regarded as condiments bearing the taint of Girl Scoutism, since it was known that no true mountain man would have been caught dead rotating a marshmallow over his blazing buffalo chips. The prospect of severe hardship, however, usually provided for a relaxation of the rules and the inclusion of a little morale-booster (the roasted marshmallow is the kid camper's peach brandy). Severe hardship was almost always prospected.

All other provisions had to be culled from the home pantry, cupboards, or refrigerator. This was known as "living off the land." The night before the expedition got underway, the young camper would enter the kitchen, gather his provisions, and depart, skillfully parrying the thrusts of his mother's broom handle with a leg of lamb. He would have tidied up the place to the point where it resembled a delicatessen looted by a Viking raiding party, and it is understandable that he would be surprised to discover that an irate troll had donned ol' Mom's clothes and was attempting to terminate his existence.

Provisioning a kid camping trip was very educational for a youngster. For one thing, it taught him the rudiments of lying. Take a typical situation. The

kid would randomly select six or seven eggs from a
dozen, boil them for exactly 135 minutes, and replace
them randomly in the carton.

"Are you sure you'll be able to tell the boiled
from the raw eggs?" his mother would ask.

"Of course," the kid would answer. Now that
would be a blatant lie. He wouldn't have the slightest
notion how to tell the boiled from the unboiled eggs.

Fortunately, this problem of the eggs always
resolved itself. By the time the camper had hauled them
over a mountain or two, he could safely assume that
all eggs that had not oozed out of the pack and down
his backside and legs were the cooked ones.

Kid camping allowed for no such effeminate
things as dehydrated or vacuum-frozen foods. It was
proof of one's manhood that he carried his food with all
the water still in it.

After an hour or so of scrounging about (or
"sacking," as some ill-tempered mothers called it) the
kitchen, the young camper would have accumulated
approximately the following provisions: a loaf of bread,
a leg of lamb, a can of condensed cream, nine slices of
bacon, a head of lettuce, a dozen eggs, a pint of salad
dressing (for the lettuce), a quart jar of cherries, a pint
of strawberry jam, three pieces of fried chicken, half a
box of corn flakes, five pounds of sugar, ten pounds of
flour, seven mealy apples, spaghetti, oatmeal, thirty-
seven grapes, a plate of fudge, a jar of peanut butter,
thirteen potatoes, a bottle of root beer, and a quart of
milk (for the corn flakes).

Once assembled, all the provisions were carefully loaded into a packsack which acquired roughly
the size, shape, and weight of an adolescent pachyderm.
Then came the moment of truth. The young camper's
jeering family would gather around to witness his at-

tempt at raising the pack clear of the sagging floor, a feat that he accomplished with a prolonged grunt which could scarcely be heard by the neighbors three houses away. He would stand there—legs spraddled and beginning to cave, shoulders slowly collapsing into the shape of a folded taco shell—and drill the disbelievers with a disdainful look from his hard, squinty eyes. And it's damned hard to make your eyes squinty when they're bugged way out like that!

Most of the adventure in kid camping came from the cooking of exotic and original dishes. Eating them was even more adventurous. Some of the dishes were undoubtedly fit for human consumption, although the sight and aroma were generally enough to give a starving and unusually indiscriminate hyena a fit of the dry heaves.

There was, of course, that old favorite: fried pork 'n' beans accented with charred potato scraps dislodged from the bottom of the serve-all skillet. This was frequently accompanied by a side order of bacon, either still flaming or recently soused with a bucket of water.

There was the aforementioned spaghetti-and-oatmeal omelet, which made an excellent dessert when topped with catsup. It is true that most of the raw eggs would have leaked away before arrival at the campsite, but usually the bottom of the pack would retain a sizable puddle, which could be augmented by the egg squeezings from the change of underwear and the extra pair of socks. These eggs had the advantage of being pre-beaten, something that cannot be said for the dehydrated kind.

It goes without saying that all dishes were

spiced with various curious, careless, and low-flying species of insects.

There was one rule of the code that no one ever mentioned but everyone adhered to, and that was that there was to be absolutely no praying on the camping trip. One time my regular fellow kid campers and I invited along a boy who lied and swore and smoked discarded cigarette butts and generally appeared to be a normal and respectable fellow. We were unutterably embarrassed by his crass display of character when, in the flicker of our dying campfire and the mirthful glow of the last bawdy joke, he knelt down by his sleeping bag, folded his hands, and said his prayers. In one fell swoop, he dealt a death blow to what otherwise showed promise of being a robust and pleasantly vulgar camping trip.

In all honesty, I must confess that I, too, once violated this particular tenet of kid camping. But I at least had the decency to do it discreetly and not in such a way as to unnerve my companions. As it happened, they were already unnerved enough.

In the middle of the night it suddenly came to our attention that a large and obviously famished bear had entered camp under the cover of darkness. He was making a terrible racket, whetting his appetite on our vast store of provisions, prior to getting on to the main course, which lay paralyzed in its sleeping bags and had all but ceased to breathe. The time had come, I realized, to invoke the aid of the Almighty, and immediately set about invoking. The next morning the other guys wrote the whole terrible affair off as a case of mistaken identity. Little did they know that it was due to my inspired efforts in our common behalf that the bear had been changed into a huge black cedar stump. The racket, they supposed, had been caused by a chipmunk assaulting a bag of potato chips. I never bothered to set them right.

Experiences like this provided the educational element in kid camping. For example, we learned that it is merely an old wives' tale that extreme fear will turn your hair snow white all over. Our hair was only a little gray about the temples, and that returned to its normal color four days later. I distinctly remember, because it was a short while after I got my voice back and just before the shaking died down to where it couldn't even be noticed from more than ten feet away.

Kid camping undoubtedly is a thing of the past, but perhaps somewhere back in the hinterlands there are a few rugged lads who practice the sport in its pure form. If there are, I must say they're mighty lucky— mighty lucky if they avoid ptomaine poisoning, permanent curvature of the spine, or growing into adults who break out in a purple rash and hysteria at the mere glimpse of a can of pork 'n' beans.

How to Fish
a Crick

🌳🌳 THERE IS MUCH CONFUSION in the world today concerning creeks and cricks. Many otherwise well-informed people live out their lives under the impression that a crick is a creek mispronounced. Nothing could be farther from the truth. A crick is a distinctly separate entity from a creek, and it should be recognized as such. After all, a creek is merely a creek, but a crick is a crick.

The extent of this confusion over cricks and creeks becomes apparent from a glance at almost any map, where you will find that all streams except rivers are labeled as creeks. There are several reasons for this injustice. First, your average run-of-the-mill cartographer doesn't know his crick from his creek. The rare cartographer who does know refuses to recognize cricks in their own right for fear that he will be chastised by one of the self-appointed chaperons of the American language, who, like all other chaperons, are big on purity.

A case in point: One of the maps I possess of the State of Washington labels a small stream as *S. Creek*. Now I don't know for certain but am reasonably sure that the actual name of this stream is not *S. No.* Just by looking at the map one can tell that it is not shaped like an *S*, the only reason I can think of for giving it such a name. *S.* therefore must not be the full name but an abbreviation. Why was the name abbreviated? Was it too long or perhaps too difficult to pronounce? Since the map also contains such stream names as Similkameen and Humptulips and Puyallup, all unabbreviated, one would guess not. This leaves only one other possibility. The cartographers felt that the actual name of the stream was obscene. They did not want it said of them that they had turned out an obscene map, the kind of map sinister characters might try to peddle to innocent school children, hissing at them from an alleyway, "Hey, kid! Wanna buy a dirty map?"

Well, I can certainly sympathize with the cartographers' reluctance to author a dirty map. What irks me is that they use the name *S. Creek*. One does not have to be a mentalist to know that the fellow who named the stream *S.* did not use the word *creek*. He used *crick*. He probably saw right off that this stream he was up was a crick and immediately started casting about for a suitable name. Then he discovered he didn't have a paddle with him. Aha! He would name this crick after the most famous of all cricks, thereby not only symbolizing his predicament but also capturing in a word something of the crick's essential character.

The cartographers in any case chose to ignore this rather obvious origin of the name and its connotations in favor of a discreet *S.* and an effete *Creek*. If they didn't want to come right out and say *crick,* why couldn't they have had the decency just to abbreviate it with a *C.* and let it go at that.

Maybe I can, once and for all, clear up this confusion over cricks and creeks.

First of all a creek has none of the raucous, vulgar, freewheeling character of a crick. If they were people, creeks would wear tuxedos and amuse themselves with the ballet, opera, and witty conversation; cricks would go around in their undershirts and amuse themselves with the Saturday-night fights, taverns, and humorous belching. Creeks would perspire and cricks, sweat. Creeks would smoke pipes; cricks, chew and spit.

Creeks tend to be pristine. They meander regally through high mountain meadows, cascade down dainty waterfalls, pause in placid pools, ripple over beds of gleaming gravel and polished rock. They sparkle in the sunlight. Deer and poets sip from creeks, and images of eagles wheel upon the surface of their mirrored depths.

Cricks, on the other hand, shuffle through cow pastures, slog through beaver dams, gurgle through culverts, ooze through barnyards, sprawl under sagging bridges, and when not otherwise occupied, thrash fitfully on their beds of quicksand and clay. Cows should perhaps be credited with giving cricks their most pronounced characteristic. In deference to the young and the few ladies left in the world whose sensitivities might be offended, I forgo a detailed description of this characteristic. Let me say only that to a cow the whole universe is a bathroom, and it makes no exception of cricks. A single cow equipped only with determination and fairly good aim

can in a matter of hours transform a perfectly good
creek into a crick.

Now that some of the basic differences between
creeks and cricks have been cleared up, I will get down
to the business at hand, namely how to fish a crick.

Every angler knows how to fish a creek. He
uses relatively light tackle and flies, and his attire consists of waders or hip boots, a fishing vest, creel, light-
weight slacks, and a shirt in a tasteful check. The creek
is worked artfully, with the fly drifting down like the
first flake of winter snow. Everybody knows that's how
you fish a creek.

But the crick, as I've pointed out, is an altogether different species of water and demands its own
particular approach.

No fancy tackle of any kind is ever used to fish
a crick. Since fiberglass rods came on the market, it is
difficult to find a good crick pole. The old steel telescope
rods were fairly good, but the best crick pole I've ever
seen was one I owned as a kid. It consisted of a six-foot
section of stiff pipe, with a piece of wire that pulled out
from the tip to provide the action. Stores sold it as a
fishing pole, but it could also serve fairly well as a lightning rod, fencepost, or a lever for prying a car out of the
mud. Rod action, it should be noted, is of little importance in crick fishing, since the crick itself usually pro-
vides about all the action one can stand.

Hook size should never be less than No. 4, and leaders, if
they are used at all, should be short and test about the
same as baling wire. This saves a good deal of time,
since if you hook up on an old log, tractor tire, or Model
T submerged in the crick, as happens every third cast,
you can simply haul it out and not have to bother

replacing leader and hook. Sinkers must be large and fat in order not to frighten off the fish. If the splash is large enough, they think it's just another old log, tractor tire, or Model T being dumped in the crick. The reel should be an old bait-caster with the worm gear busted and the handle off. A crick reel, if you don't happen to own one, can be improvised by loaning a perfectly good creek reel to one of your kids for a period of one to five minutes.

The experienced crick fisher never wears hip boots or waders on a crick. Old oxfords with flappy tongues are all right, but tennis shoes in the final stages of decay are the first choice of crick fishers everywhere. Whatever shoes you select, they should have sizable holes both fore and aft. The holes allow for good circulation of the crick water through the shoe and help to cut down on the risk of fermentation of the feet. Another advantage is that the crick fisher can thrust his toes out through the holes and get a good grip on banks of submerged clay, rotting logs, old tractor tires, and Model T's.

The creel is shunned in crick fishing. All fish are carried on a forked stick, which adds immeasurably to the enjoyment of the sport. Most of this enjoyment comes from laying the forked stick down, forgetting it, and then spending several happy hours looking for it. Once the crick fisher tires of this pastime he usually vows to keep the stick in hand at all times. This brings into play the ultimate in crick-fishing skill, since the angler must now land his fish by taking up his slack line with his teeth and one ear, accomplished by a quick, dipping, circular motion of the head.

Flies, of course, are never used on a crick. The crick fish just gaffaw at them. They want real meat—fat, wiggling worms, grasshoppers on the hoof, and, occasionally, toes.

That pretty much covers the technique of crick fishing. Naturally one cannot expect to master it so quickly as creek fishing, unless, of course, he happens to be under the age of fourteen. Eight-year-olds are naturals at crick fishing, and if you have one handy you might take him out to a crick and observe him in action. Despite the opinion of all parents and most behavioral psychologists, eight-year-olds are good for something, and teaching the art of crick fishing is it.

At least once a year I try to fish Sand Crick, the crick of my youth. Admittedly, I have lost a good deal of my technique and most of my stamina but I still manage to have a good time. Usually I come back with a few fish, some good laughs, and a charley horse that extends from my trapezius to my peroneus longus.

Last summer my cousin Buck accompanied me, and I got one of those terrible scares that only crick fishing can give you. We had no more than started when Buck stepped into quicksand. It startled him so badly that he could only manage to get off three or four casts before total panic set in. The quicksand by then was halfway up to his knees.

"Hey," Buck said. "I don't think I'll be able to get out."

A cold chill shot through me. Not only was a lifelong friend and relative in peril but he was carrying the communal worm can.

"Quick," I yelled. "Toss me the worm can!"

"Nothing doing," Buck said. "Not till you drag me out of here."

I wasted a good ten minutes of fishing time getting him out of that quicksand. On the other hand, I probably would have used up more time than that digging a new batch of worms besides having to knock off a little early to tell his wife there was no point in waiting supper on him.

Incidentally, in order to prevent a similar emergency from occurring, I took the precaution of putting a handful of worms in my shirt pocket, where they were eventually discovered by my wife on washday. It is interesting to note that dehydrated worms cannot be reconstituted by even three cycles in an automatic washer. Also of interest is the fact that it is almost as difficult to reconstitute the wife who conducts the experiment. After such an occurrence, the wise though absentminded crick fisher should take care to eat all his meals out for several days, and in the unlikely event that the wife does offer him something to eat, he should first give a bite to the dog and observe the animal carefully for a couple of hours afterwards.

Buck and I fished a couple of miles of Sand Crick together that day, reminiscing every step of the way over our adventures as kids along this same crick. We came upon a half-submerged car, a 1937 Packard that someone had dumped in the crick under the pretext of preventing bank erosion but actually to be rid of a 1937 Packard. Buck drifted his line in through the gaping holes of the front windshield and hooked a fine Eastern brook out of the back seat.

"First time I ever caught anything in the back seat of a 1937 Packard," he said.

"I've never been that lucky," I said enviously, "but I came pretty close once in a '48 Hudson."

The last hole of the day was one known affectionately as The Dead Cow Hole. The particular cow that the hole was named after was one of the most malicious beasts ever to deface the banks of a crick. I don't know what the farmer called his cow but I know some of the names fishermen called her, always preceded by the same presumably accurate adjective. You always knew when a fellow planned on fishing the stretch of crick presided over by the cow, because he carried his fishing pole in one hand and an ax handle in the other. (Usually you could get in at least one good blow each time the cow galloped over the top of you.) Then one day the cow took ill and died, thus, or so I thought, effectively removing herself from action. The news reached me on a sweltering summer day, but nevertheless I made ready immediately to take advantage of the cow's misfortune. I scarcely touched the tops of the withered grass in my rush to get a line in the water.

As I neared the crick, however, I noticed a flock of magpies flying hurriedly in the opposite direction, and several of them, I observed, showed definite signs of nausea. At about the same time a hot, dry gust of wind criminally assaulted my olfactory nerves with such violence as to bring tears to my eyes.

"No!" I thought. "Could it be? Could she actually have been that fiendish?" The question was shortly answered in the affirmative. On peering down from the top of the hill above the crick, I could see her carcass ripening in the summer heat not ten yards from the fishing hole!

Evidently she had seen the end coming and rather than spend her last moments repenting her sins she had, with malice aforethought, used them to drag herself into a strategic position so that, even in death, she would dominate not only the immediate area of the fishing hole but four-hundred yards on all sides.

Several times I took a deep breath and tried to rush the hole but my wind always gave out before I could cover the distance. It was hopeless, at least for me. Cousin Buck did manage to fish Dead Cow Hole that same summer, and with considerable success apparently. He told me about it a week later and I believe he said he caught a couple of good fish. I couldn't be sure because he was still gagging so hard it was difficult to understand him.

That's the nature of crick fishing, though. Some people may not have the heart for it, or even the stomach, but for those who do, it has its rewards. They escape me at the moment, however.

Further Teachings of Rancid Crabtree

GRAM SLICED OFF four great slabs from a loaf of her homemade bread. She spread them with butter, piled on a couple pounds of ham, slices of onions, pickles, cheese, and the leftovers from the previous night's supper. Then she stuffed the sandwiches in a paper bag and thrust them into my hands.

"But I tell you I don't need food," I protested. "Rancid is going to teach me how to live off the land."

"Shoot," my grandmother said, waving a butcher knife at me. "That old fool don't know any more about livin' off the land than he does about workin'. Now take those sandwiches and don't give me any sass."

On my way over to Rancid's cabin, I stuffed the sandwiches down the front of my shirt, hoping he wouldn't notice I was carrying contraband.

"What you hidin' thar?" the old mountain man

said the instant he caught sight of me. "You got a water-melon under yer shart?"

"Naw," I answered, embarrassed. "Gram made me bring along a couple of sandwiches in case I got hungry."

Rancid hooted. "Thet ol' widder woman, when she gonna cut you loose from her apron strings and let you be a man?"

"I don't know," I said. "I told her you were going to teach me how to live off the land, but she pulled a knife and made me take the sandwiches anyway."

"Yup, she's a mean-un, all right," Rancid said. "Wall, them samwiches won't hurt nothin, and might come in handy in case we has an emargency."

I should explain that Gram and Rancid were natural enemies. Gram possessed all the qualities Rancid despised in a person. She was practical, hard-working, neat, clean, methodical, and never smoked, drank, or told lies. "She ain't hoomin," Rancid often complained. Gram claimed Rancid was the only person she had ever known who was totally lacking in charac-ter. By "character" she meant a tendency toward work. A man could rustle cows, steal chickens, and rob banks in his spare time, and Gram would say of him, "Rufus may have some bad ways, but I'll tell you this, he's a *good worker*. He ain't totally no good like some folks by the name of Rancid Crabtree I could mention, but I won't."

To Gram, being a good worker excused a lot of shortcomings, but it wasn't the sort of lifestyle that ap-pealed to me at the age of twelve. Since Rancid was the only person I'd ever known who hadn't once been caught redhanded in an act of holding a job, I figured he must have some secret, and I studied him the way

other kids in school studied their arithmetic. Because he
didn't work, Rancid always had time to give you, not
just little pinched-off minutes but hours and days and
even whole weeks. He was a fine example for a kid to
pattern himself after.

On this particular day, Rancid and I were going to hike
back in the mountains and spend the night in a lean-to
we would build ourselves. All we would take with us
were some fishline and hooks, some twine and our
knives, and, as it turned out, the two four-pound sandwiches. The morning was one of those impeccable speci-
mens found only in early July in the Rocky Mountains,
particularly when it is only the twelfth July you have
known in your life. That was back in the old days before
environment had been discovered, and there were only
trees and blue sky and water moving swift and clear.
Hiking along behind the lean old woodsman, I listened
to the soft humming of summer and paid attention to
keeping my toes pointed Indian fashion as I spashed
through the shallow pools of sunlight on the trail. It was
a very pleasant day to start learning how to live off the
land so I would never have to work.

We hiked hard for the first hour to shake off
the last lingering shards of civilization, and then slowed
our paces as the trail began winding up into the mountains. Far down below in the patchwork of fields, we
could see the farmers wrestling with their hay crops.
We laughed.

After a while, Rancid started giving me living-
off-the-land lessons. The first thing he had me do was
to smear my face with mud.

"This hyar mud will keep off the moss-kee-
toos," Rancid explained.

I smeared on a copious quantity of mud, because if there was one thing in the world I was interested in keeping off, it was moss-kee-toos. I had heard plenty about moss-kee-toos from Rancid before. They were vicious flying creatures that sometimes would swarm out of the woods and suck the blood from your body. Since I had spent a good deal of time in the woods and never seen a moss-kee-too, I hoped they were merely a figment of Rancid's imagination. (His imagination was crammed with all sorts of weird and interesting figments.) If moss-kee-toos did exist, the mud did a good job of keeping them off. It even worked pretty well on the mosquitoes.

Another rare creature apparently known only to Rancid was the iggle. He pointed to a large bird circling high above the mountain peak. "Look thar, boy! Thas a iggle." The bird was too high for me to make out any of its features, but in the years since, I have frequently seen high-flying birds that I assumed to be iggles, so I'm pretty sure they exist. Rancid told me that iggles were so big they often carried off half-grown cows in their claws, and as a result were not much loved by ranchers. "But hell," he said, "iggles got a right to a livin' too."

Rancid had his own system of ornithological classification. There were three basic groups of birds: little birds, medium-sized birds, and big birds. A few birds were referred to by their common names: ducks, doves, grouse, pheasants, and iggles. Rancid's system of ornithology worked just as well on identifying rarer birds.

"What's that bird?" I would ask Rancid.

"Thet thar is what ya calls yer little black-and-white bird with a red head," he would tell me authoritatively. I never ceased to marvel at how Rancid knew all the different kinds of birds. Just by looking at them you could tell he knew what he was talking about.

Along about noon I began to feel the first pangs of hunger. I suggested to Rancid that maybe the time had come for us to knock off the nature study and start living off the land and if it wasn't too much trouble I'd like to take a look at the lunch menu. Rancid looked around the land.

"Ah figured we'd have huckleburries fer lunch, but they's still green. The wild razzburries should be ripe up in the meadows, though. Fer the time bein', whyn't you give me one of them samwiches yer granny packed?"

"Who do you take me for, Mother Nature?" I said angrily. "You're supposed to teach me how to live off the land."

"Don't gitcher tail in a knot," Rancid said. "Livin' off the land takes a powerful lot of thinkin', and ah thinks better if ah'm chompin' on a samwich. Now what did thet ol' widder woman fix us?"

We split one of the sandwiches, and sure enough, Rancid started thinking better. "As soon as we gets done with lunch, we better find us some mushrooms to cook with our game for supper. Thar's a burn up ahead and we kin probably find some mushrooms thar."

I was a bit worried about the mushrooms, since my grandmother had told me Rancid didn't know his fungi from a hole in the ground.

"Gram says one good way to tell if a mushroom ain't poisonous is to see if the deer have been eating them," I offered.

"Thet's the dumbest thing ah ever hear'd tell of," Rancid said with disgust. "Deer don't know much more than yer granny does. Mushrooms is little wrinkled pointy things, and toadstools is all the rest. Deer eat toadstools all the time and it don't bother 'em none. A hoomin bean eat a toadstool, the fust thang he knows he's knockin' on the Parly Gate with one hand and still pickin' his teeth with t' other."

Fortunately, we were unable to find any mushrooms in the burn, although I did happen to come across a patch of little wrinkled pointy things not worth the trouble of calling to Rancid's attention.

The raspberries in the high mountain meadow were ripe, as Rancid had predicted, but not especially plentiful. Nevertheless, I got a keen sense of living off the land from eating them. Rancid explained at considerable length how to pick and eat wild raspberries, and seemed very pleased with himself. "Lots of folks don't know wild razzburries is good to eat," he said. I personally had never encountered anyone who didn't know they were good to eat, but I didn't say anything.

"Gram says even cattails are good to eat," I offered.

"Ha!" Rancid laughed. "Thet silly ol' woman, it's a wonder she's lived to be a hunnert and five, what with all her notions about eatin' pisonous plants."

"I don't think she's that old," I said.

"Thet just goes to show you," Rancid said. "Now don't let me hear no more of thet talk about eatin' cattails."

Next Rancid showed me how to set snares for rabbits, an absolute essential for anyone intending to live off the land. Although I knew the basic principle and technology of snares, I never quite understood how you induced the game to stick his head into the loop and trigger the contraption.

"How do you know the rabbit is going to run

into the snare?" I asked, peering intently over Rancid's shoulder as he worked. "He's got a million other places to run."

"Wall, fust of all, you have to be smarter than the rabbit," he said with a chuckle. "You got to be smarter than the rabbit. Now hep me move these logs and rocks. What we is gonna do is funnel thet ol' rabbit right into our snare, see?"

We dragged rocks and logs and tree limbs and brush and piled them up in a giant open-ended V that pointed right at the snare. By the time the V was finished, both of us were so hot and tired we were staggering, but I didn't complain because I was learning how to live off the land so I would never ever have to work.

After we had rested a while, Rancid said, "Now hyar's what you do. You climb down behind thet thicket over thar and make a racket so that you drive the rabbits into the funnel."

"How come we both don't climb down and make a racket?" I asked.

" 'Cause ah have to sit on thet log up thar and shoosh any rabbits thet come thet way back into the snare."

"Why can't I do that and you drive the rabbits out?"

Rancid thought a moment, mopping the sweat off his face with his shirt sleeve. "You had any experience shooshing wild rabbits?"

"No."

"Wall, thar you are! Now git yerself down in the thicket and start making a racket."

"A half-hour later I emerged from the thicket. Rancid was sitting on the log, his elbows resting on his

knees, staring vacantly down at the snare. "How . . .
pant . . . big a one . . . *pant pant* . . . did we catch?"
I asked, sinking to the ground.

Rancid rolled a chaw of tobacco around in his
cheek. "Wall, ah kin say one thang about these
blankety-blank rabbits. They is powerful smart!"

"You mean to say we didn't catch any?"

"What would you think about chompin' down
some nice tender trout roasted over a fahr?" Rancid
said brightly. "Don't thet sound good!"

Early in the afternoon we arrived at a little lake
tucked away between two mountain peaks. Rancid cut
two willow poles and tied fishline to them. Then we
started looking around for grubs to bait the hooks with.
As Rancid said, you can never find a grub when you
really need one. Savagely, we tore apart rotted logs
looking for grubs, the essential link between us and a
fish supper. I was beginning to think working might be
easier than living off the land.

At last we found a small deposit of grubs,
tossed them into Rancid's hat and hurried back down to
the lake. By the time we got there, the grubs were
choking and gagging but otherwise in good shape. The
trout brazenly committed grand larceny on most of our
bait supply but we managed to land a couple of
eight-inchers.

"Now ah'm gonna show you how to build a fahr without
matches," Rancid said. He made a little bow-and-stick
contraption of the sort I had seen in my Boy Scout handbook. The handbook, however, had not indicated all
the good words you were supposed to say in order to get
a fire going. Rancid sawed the little bow furiously back
and forth on the stick, the spinning of which was supposed to ignite a little pile of shavings. It was all very

complicated, and Rancid sweated and panted and swore until his eyes bugged out even more than usual. At last a little curl of smoke drifted up from the shavings. Rancid threw down the bow, dropped on his belly and started blowing on the shavings, whereupon the curl of smoke instantly vanished. He rolled over on his back and crumpled the bow and stick in his hands. "Let this be a lesson to you, boy. Don't never go out in the woods without a fistful of matches."

"That's what Gram told me," I said. "She made me bring a bunch of matches even though I told her we wouldn't be needing them."

"Gol-dang know-it-all ol' woman! Gimmie one of them matches!"

In a second Rancid had a fire going. His hands were shaking from exhaustion and rage as he built a little willow grill to cook our fish on. As the flames licked around the two little trout, Rancid stared moodily into the fire.

"When we gonna build the lean-to?" I asked.

"Don't bother me about no lean-to," he growled. He seemed a bit surly, so I decided not to pursue the subject.

Then the two fish slipped through the grill into the fire. I stepped back, sneaking a glance at Rancid's face. His eyes, widening slightly, stared at the bits of blackened skin on the willow grill. A tiny quiver ran the length of his lower lip.

After a long moment of silence, Rancid said, "We best eat thet last samwich, 'cause we is gonna need lots of energy."

"To build the lean-to?" I asked.

"No," he said. "So we kin walk real fast. Ah figures if we leave now we kin get back to yer house in time for supper."

"Gram said she'd set a couple places for us," I

said, "even though I tried to tell her we'd be gone all night."

"Thet ol' know-it-all," Rancid said. "Ah wonder what's she's fixin' fer supper anyhow. Ah shore hope it ain't gonna be a mess of pisonous cattails!"

The Great
Cow Plot

WHEN I CAME IN from fishing the other day, my wife asked, "Have any luck?"

"Great," I said. "I saw only two cows and got away from both of them."

I hadn't caught any fish, but that was beside the point. The success or failure of my fishing trips depends not upon the size of the catch but the number of cows encountered.

Some people do most of their fishing on lakes or the ocean, where cows are seldom if ever encountered. Most of my fishing is done in cow pastures, the natural habitat of cows.

Even when I plan a fishing trip forty miles back into the wilderness a herd of cows will usually get wind of it and go on a forced march to get there before I do and turn the place into a cow pasture. Sometimes the cows get the word a little late, and I'll pass them on the way. Invariably a few of the poor losers will gallop along in front of the car, still trying to get there ahead of me and do what they can on short notice and empty stomachs.

"I've given up hope of finding any place to fish where a cow won't manage to show up and put in her oar. If I was in the pet shop on the nineteenth floor of a department store and stopped to net a guppy out of an aquarium, a cow would get off the elevator and rush over to offer advice.

My wife insists that I've become paranoiac from overexposure to cows. She tries to tell me that the intricate and near-impenetrable patterns of cow spoor laid down around my favorite fishing holes are a result of nothing more than random chance. Even granting high probability from the number of placements per square yard, which is altogether ample, I remain unconvinced that these bovine mine fields are not the product of conspiracy and cunning. There's probably a small island in the Caribbean where cows are given a six-week course in the design and manufacture of mine fields before being turned out to pasture alongside fine trout streams. The whole thing is a plot by Castro to lower our national morale.

All cows are fishing enthusiasts, although their idea of fishing might better be described as "Chase the Fisherman." The object of the sport is to see how many times the fisherman can be made to cross the creek. Five points are earned if he wades across, ten points if he splashes only once, and twenty-five if he hurls himself across without touching the water. The last is achieved by first running him twice around the pasture to pick up momentum and then making a straight shot for the creek. This maneuver is usually good for a score, providing the fisherman can be driven past the other team's goalie.

As fishing enthusiasts, cows can be divided roughly into two groups: participants and *aficionados.* Another grouping I find useful is simply Fast Mean Cows (FMC) and Slow Mean Cows (SMC). The SMC, mediocre athletes at best, are usually content to watch the main events between the FMC and fishermen (thus the expression "contented cows"). They participate only to the extent of doing everything in their power to ruin an otherwise good running turf, apparently in the belief that a slow field improves the spectator sport. The FMC are frequently referred to as "bulls." The term is usually preceded by harsh but accurately descriptive adjectives. It is sometimes argued that "bulls" is not an appropriate term for FMC since some of them are known to give milk. I disagree. Upon hearing the shout "Here comes a ——— bull!" I have yet to see any of my companions wait around to argue over the sex of the beast.

No effective cow repellent has ever been developed for the comfort of fishermen. Simply from the standpoint of size alone, one would think that cow repellent would have priority over mosquito repellent. I don't know if it would work, but someone with a knack for chemistry might try distilling and bottling the aroma of a well-done sirloin.

The only thing that bulls have any respect for at all is the stick, and many knowledgeable cow-pasture fishermen carry one slipped under their belt for easy access in an emergency. This is known as the "bull stick" or sometimes simply "BS." When the bull approaches, the BS is first waved threateningly in the air and then thrown. (This is not to be confused with the BS thrown by hunters.)

A couple of fishermen I know like to brag about their narrow escape from a grizzly bear, *Ursus horribilis,* but I'm not impressed. A man just hasn't done any real escaping until he has escaped from a grizzly cow, *Bovinus horribilis.* I am probably the world's leading authority on the subject, having studied it since my childhood days.

In my mind's eyes, now somewhat astigmatic but Wide Screen and Tru-Color, I see myself as a young boy, fishing pole in one hand, worm can in the other, making my way down to the creek. My phlegmatic and flatulent old dog, Stranger, is close upon my bare heels and close upon his heels is our neighbor's bull, known in those parts as The Bull, and we are all running to beat hell. Stranger, his jaws set in a grim smile, runs between me and The Bull not out of any sense of loyalty or protection but because of old age and a shortness of breath. Arriving at the fence the dog and I hurl ourselves into the sanctuary beyond and The Bull screeches to a stop in a cloud of dust and slobber just short of the wire. Stranger, sweat streaming down his face, pulls himself together long enough to take credit for once again having saved my life—"Well, bailed you out of another bad spot didn't I?"—and then he and The Bull stand on opposite sides of the fence and say cruel and obscene things to each other while I ignore them and get on with the day's fishing.

Why did I risk frequent confrontations with such a malevolent creature as The Bull? The reason is one that perhaps only a trout fisherman would understand. Little Sand Creek was a great trout stream, probably one of the finest in the nation at that time, but with the humility of all the truly great it meandered its regal course through a series of humble and unpretentious—not to say miserable—farms, one of which was ours. The stream was fished with such ardor and love and perseverance by so many anglers that by mid-season any worthwhile trout who had survived the onslaught would strike at nothing that did not show obvious signs of life and then only after taking its pulse. That section of the stream which ran through the farm owned and operated by The Bull, however, remained virtually untouched—except, of course, by me, known affectionately throughout the region as "That Fool Kid."

These sorties across the pasture were not nearly so hazardous as the chance observer might suppose. The Bull's top speed was a good deal faster than mine, no doubt because he didn't have to carry a fishing rod and a can of worms or worry about his dog's heart. But we had the element of surprise on our side, and by the time The Bull caught sight of us we already would be well accelerated. If The Bull closed the gap too quickly, I would jettison rod and worms, and Stranger would jettison everything he could, and we would give it our all, every man for himself, right up to the fence, and hurl ourselves over, under or through the barbed wires. Such instances were rare, however, and most of the time we could get through the fence in a manner that was more dignified and much less painful.

I learned a great deal about plane geometry from these exercises with The Bull. I discovered that the shortest distance between two points is a straight line, an idea that The Bull either could not fathom or he was reading Einsteinian theory in his spare time. At any rate, he almost always ran in a long, arching curve. This resulted from his knowing nothing about leading a moving target; he always held dead on. Consequently, a diagram of our converging lines of motion would show his course as a long curved line intersecting and merging with my short straight line. Successful evasion thus was largely a matter of predicting, given the proper angles, distances, relative speeds, and variable handicaps, the point at which our two converging lines of motion would intersect. As I say, I was a master of such calculations. My talent went wholly unrecognized, however, and people continued to refer to me as "That Fool Kid."

It came to pass that my widowed mother took up with a man and married him, offering the feeble excuse that "the boy needed a father." Both she and I knew that was an out-and-out lie. She had pulled off a clever coup d'etat, designed to deprive me of my place of power and authority over the family, which I had been ruling with a firm but just hand since the age of eight. The mercenary imported to depose me proved to be a tough customer, and I saw that I would have to play it cool and watch for the main chance. It came sooner than I expected. Hank, as he was called, one morning sent a peace feeler in my direction: "Don't know of a spot where we could catch some fish, do you?" he asked.

Well, it seemed like no time at all before the mercenary and I were standing at the fence to The Bull's pasture. I thought it best to warn him. "That ol' cow out there seems to be lookin' our way," I said.

"That ain't no cow," the mercenary said. "That's a bull. But land, boy, you don't have to be afraid of a bull. All you gotta do is show 'im who's boss."

It seemed a comfort to him to see me smile, the first time since being deposed. What he didn't notice was that Stranger and The Bull were smiling too. It became kind of an "in" joke, afterwards. That is, after the mercenary had climbed through the fence and demonstrated to all of us just who was boss. It turned out that the boss was just exactly who I and Stranger and The Bull had known all along was boss.

The mercenary, we smugly observed, wasn't much of a hand at fighting bulls. On the other hand, he proved to be the best broken-field runner ever to hit our county. To this day I have never seen a grown man who could run so fast, even one who wasn't carrying a fishing rod and creel, and wearing hipboots. A kid just had to admire a man who could run like that.

From then on Hank and I and Stranger ran from The Bull together, and we went far afield and ran from other bulls and sometimes cows and even whole herds of cows, and we forgot all about power and authority and the like. We were willing to risk the wrath of any cow who stood guard over a stretch of good fishing water, and it wasn't long before we were being referred to as "That Fool Kid and That Fool Man." But we paid her no mind; she had her hands full, what with being the head of the family and all.

The Mountain Man

MY CHIEF CAREER AMBITION as a youngster was to be a mountain man, but somehow it never worked out. I'm not sure why.

One problem was my family. They were dead set against the idea of my going into the fur trade, and never passed up an opportunity to point out the drawbacks of the profession.

My grandmother had actually known some real mountain men back in the old days, but she had never taken a liking to them. She said they drank and swore and spit tobacco and never took baths and fought and bragged and lied all the time. I don't recall, however, that she ever mentioned what was bad about them.

"There ain't no money in bein' a mountain man," Gram would tell me. She was fond of pointing out that she had never known a mountain man who was the proprietor of the basest vessel of domesticity and personal hygiene. Her exact words escape me at the moment.

I was all for leaving school and getting started in the fur trade as soon as possible, but my mother wouldn't hear of it. She said I would have to wait until I was through the third grade or reached the age of eighteen, whichever came first. "It's the law," she would say. The suggestion was put forth that we might find a loophole in the law if we looked hard enough, but Mom said she didn't think it was proper for a third-grade teacher to be putting forth suggestions like that.

My older sister, who liked to boast that she knew how to turn small boys into frogs and offered me as evidence, was always there to put in her oar and rile the waters of argument.

"You can't be a mountain man," she would say. "You're afraid of the dark."

Well, I certainly didn't see how she knew so much about what mountain men were afraid of and what they weren't. There were probably plenty of mountain men who were afraid of the dark, even though the length of their expeditions into the wilderness may have been somewhat limited by the handicap. One could easily imagine a grizzled old trapper asking, "Any sign of beaver a half-day's ride from the fort?"

In spite of these difficulties, I persisted in preparing myself for a career in the mountain man profession. Every spare moment was spent either in the library extracting the theory from books or out in the woods conducting laboratory experiments.

One thing I learned from the books was that a mountain man had to master three basic skills if he wanted to survive in the wilds. He had to know how to squint his eyes just right, spit through his teeth, and say dry, humorous things anytime he was in pain or danger. (You'd be surprised how difficult it is to think of something dry and humorous to say when, for example, a big furry beast is eating one of your legs.) Much time was spent perfecting squinting and spitting, and I learned that it's easy to say dry if not humorous things after one has spent the day spitting through his teeth.

I had at my disposal about forty-seven rusty traps, which I kept in a neat snarl in our woodshed. From time to time, I would go out and practice setting these traps. It almost never failed that the practice session would end with a trap snapping shut on one portion or another of my anatomy. Now it was part of the mountain man code that you could never cry when caught by one of your own traps, but there was no rule against doing as much loud yelling as you wanted, particularly if you were a mountain man who didn't know how to swear well enough to do a trapped finger much good. Quite often I would become confused on these occasions and go about for some time afterwards squinting my teeth and spitting through my eyes. I could always think of something dry and humorous to say, but it was usually about three days later, and I wasn't sure if that counted.

Besides the traps, I practiced a lot with snares. Since beavers seldom if ever passed through our yard, I impressed my crotchety old dog, Strange, into service. I would rig up a snare outside his house, where he would be sleeping off a night of drunken debauchery. Then I would raise some kind of racket until he staggered out asking for tomato juice and a little peace and quiet, and the snare would close limply around his neck. He would curse me roundly and lunge back into his den of iniquity, dragging the snare with him to be chewed up at his leisure and when his stomach felt better.

The only deadfall I ever constructed utilized an old railroad tie and almost ended the promising career of one of my mother's laying hens. The hen survived the ordeal, but for some time we had the distinction of owning the only flat chicken in the neighborhood. I exhausted my entire supply of ingenuity proposing theories about how a four-pound chicken could manage to crawl under a hundred-pound railroad tie. To this day I'm not sure how she could have triggered the contraption, unless perhaps she was standing under it running tests on the engineering.

One area of information about mountain men that caused me a good deal of confusion was buffalo chips. From my extensive reading on the subject, I knew that mountain men preferred this fuel above all others. The books never came right out and said what buffalo chips were, nor did they give any recommendations about the proper procedure for chipping a buffalo. One thing for certain, it would be dang hard work chipping one of the ornery critters. It was no wonder to me that buffalo were all the time stampeding the way they did, what with mountain men constantly hacking their fuel supply off of them.

When I eventually learned the true nature of buffalo chips, I could scarcely believe it. I had known all along that mountain men were tough but not just how tough.

Most mountain men died off back in the nineteenth century, once again displaying their uncommon good sense but also depriving students of the profession, such as myself, of live models to pattern themselves after. From time to time, someone would attempt to pass himself off to me as a mountain man, but I always found him out. One of these impostors was my older cousin Buck, who was big and husky and had perfected all the mannerisms of the mountain man. He was a good squinter and spitter and spoke mountain man passingly well. He liked to say things like, "Fetch us some water, ol' hoss, and ah'll build us a fahr and bile up some coffee."

For a long time, Buck had me fooled. Then one day we went fishing up Hoodoo Canyon, a place that is spooky even in daylight. We fooled around most of the day, catching a few trout, poking at tracks, studying bent blades of grass, squinting and spitting, saying dry, humorous things, and the like, and before I knew it, I had broken a long-standing promise to myself, which was never to get caught up in Hoodoo Canyon after dark. I comforted myself with the thought that I was in the company of a trained and knowledgeable mountain man. Then I glimpsed Buck's face. I knew without having to ask that he had just broken a long-standing promise to himself.

We started picking our way down the overgrown trail at a pace Buck referred to as a dogtrot, even though I personally have never been acquainted with a dog that could trot that fast. As we dogtrotted along, leaping logs four feet in the air without having to speed up, I began to get the impression we were being followed. Buck received the report of this news with no great enthusiasm, but he stopped to size up the situation. After all, if you are being tracked by something large and hairy, it's a good idea to know how large and how hairy. Every true mountain man knows that the worst thing you can do is let your imagination drive you into a panic. You want to look at your situation coldly and realistically, and that's exactly what Buck and I were doing when a long, cold and very realistic scream drifted down off the mountain above us. As sounds go, it registered right up near the top of the hideous scale.

(The only time I had heard anything like it was when a small, harmless snake managed to sneak into our house and hide in the drawer where my sister kept her underwear.)

"Whazzat?" I asked, attempting to feign idle curiosity.

Buck was silent. Then, drawing upon his vast knowledge, he identified the sound.

. "That was a blinkety-blank *scream!*" he said, thereby confirming my worst suspicions.

No more had this been said than there was the sound of a large animal bolting off down the canyon, snapping off young lodgepole pine like they were matchsticks, bounding over huge logs, smashing its way blindly through thickets, snorting, grunting, and wheezing for all it was worth. It took several seconds before I realized the large animal was Buck.

Although I was fully sympathetic with his motives, I simply could not accept Buck's undignified departure from Hoodoo Canyon as being consistent with the calm, cool manner of a mountain man. His abandoning of his loyal partner in a time of danger was also a serious infraction of the rules. That the loyal partner, despite a late start and short legs, managed to beat him out of the mouth of the canyon by a good forty yards in no way mitigated the offense, at least in my judgment.

My early training as a mountain man has stood me in good stead over all the years I've spent prowling about the wilds on one pretext or another. But in the end, I failed to become a full-time, card-carrying mountain man. The obstacles seemed to increase as the years went by, and there's no question that a mountain man today would have a hard time of it. First of all, he would have difficulty finding a mountain unadorned with ski lodges, condominiums, television towers, and the like. Then he would have to carry a briefcase for all his licenses, registrations, permits, draft and social security cards, health insurances and so on, and that would take a lot of the fun out of it. There would be all the hassles with the fish and game departments, and the Forest Service would be forever flying over and spraying him with one kind of pesticide or another. The USFS recreation officers would probably hound him to use the prepared campsites for his own safety (he might get himself clearcut up on the mountains), and providing he could even find a few buffalo chips to ignite, he would have to run the risk of getting doused with a bomber load of fire retardant.

It's probably just as well that I never became a mountain man. Still, some days on the streets of the city, dodging stampedes of taxis and herds of muggers, squinting my eyes just right against the smog, sidestepping dog chips, and all the time trying to think of something dry and humorous to say, I frequently wonder where I went wrong.

The Rescue

THERE ARE PEOPLE who constantly look as if they are in dire need of help. I am one of them.

Men, women and children, and even scraggly dogs are forever coming up to me to ask if they might be of some assistance. I don't mind if I'm in some sort of real trouble. Usually, though, my predicament is nothing more serious than waiting on a street corner for the light to change, or perhaps trying to look disinterested while the service station attendant tries to remember what he did with the key.

Once I was standing in front of a candy-vending machine, trying to decide between a Nut Crunchy and a Whang-O Bar. A pert young lady came up and asked if she might be of service. I said no, that I had already decided on a Whang-O. You could tell from the look on her face that she was disappointed at having arrived too late to help with the decision. If I'm not mistaken, she went off in a bit of a huff.

Even when I'm at home people are constantly offering me aid and comfort. The other morning I was staring vacantly out the window, a hobby I personally find more entertaining than, say, stamp collecting or golf.

"What's the matter?" my wife asked.

"Nothing," I said. "Why?"

"You're staring vacantly out the window." Her tone suggested that this is an activity engaged in only by persons on the verge of leaping feet first into the garbage disposal. "What's the matter?"

In order to bring a brief but merciful end to the discussion, I made up a mildly risque cock-and-bull story about a premonition, the villain of which was a sadistic crocodile.

"But why do you keep staring out the window like that?" she persisted.

"I'm watching for the SOB!" I told her.

Not only am I not free to stare vacantly out one of my own windows, I'm afraid even to go outside and lie down on my own grass. If I did, one of the neighbors would call an ambulance for me or, worse yet (with a couple of notable exceptions), rush over and try to give me mouth-to-mouth resuscitation.

Now that's the sort of thing that happens to me around my own home, on city streets, and in office buildings. If I wander anywhere off the beaten paths, my would-be rescuers become so numerous they have to circle me in holding patterns in order to await their turns.

When a hunter meets another hunter in the woods, he will usually greet him with some inoffensive remark like, "Any luck?" or "How ya doin'?" and let it go at that. With me, other hunters instantly assume I am lost, injured, or being sought by the Mafia. They launch into intricate directions on how I can make my way to the nearest road, hospital, or hiding place. If I didn't deal somewhat firmly with them, they would boil me a pot of soup, set my leg in a splint, and carry me piggy-back to my car.

Even my hunting partners of long years standing are quick to assume that if I'm out of sight, I'm lost. Such an assumption is entirely unfounded. Occasionally I will discover that a road or trail or mountain is not where I last left it, but that is not my fault. If a mountain wishes to change its location, there is nothing I can do to prevent it.

On a hunting trip a few years ago I spent most of the day looking for a road that had mysteriously moved. Upon finding another road, I made my way down to the highway and walked to the nearest diner, where I ordered myself a steak dinner. No sooner had I been served than one of my hunting partners burst into the diner and shouted that he needed some men for a search party to look for some poor devil who was lost in the mountains. I immediately made my steak into a sandwich and stood up to offer my services. It turned out I was the fellow I was supposed to search for. Such incidents are embarrassing.

I should like to make clear here that I am no more incompetent or susceptible to trouble than the average person, no matter what my friends might say. I have managed pretty much on my own to survive a big-league depression, numerous recessions, creeping inflations, and even a couple of phases. I have never been tested in military combat, but I did spend several years teaching English composition to college freshmen. As a police reporter, I had experiences that would give a grave robber goose bumps and a hungry hyena a fit of the dry heaves. I offer this bit of personal history as evi-

dence that I am not totally helpless and inexperienced;
I just look that way.

From years of almost constant rescuing I have arrived
at the firm conviction that if one can possibly avoid
being rescued he should by all means do so. As a rule,
suffering the consequences of one's predicament is
preferable to the risks of being rescued.

One day last summer I had fished a couple of
miles of mountain stream and was just starting to hoof
it back up the road to my car when a pickup truck
pulled up alongside and stopped. Two men and a
woman were in the front seat. A load of firewood was
stacked high in the back of the truck.

"You look plumb wore out," one of them said
despite the fact that I felt quite fresh and vigorous, and
was enjoying the little hike. "Hop onto the wood back
there and we'll give you a lift."

The speaker was one of those burly, broad-
shouldered types—unshaven, voice like a bass drum, and
hard, squinty eyes. The two men weren't exactly cream-
puffs either. I knew they would brook no nonsense about
my declining to be rescued, so I climbed up on top the
firewood. The wood was split into large chunks, each of
which was equipped with an abundance of edges approximately as sharp as the blade of a skinning knife.
I eased myself down on the fewest number possible, attempting through an act of will to keep most of my
weight suspended in air.

Now almost everyone knows that it is impossible to drive a pickup load of firewood sixty miles an
hour over a washboard road. The driver of the truck
proved to be one of the few persons in the world not in
possession of this knowledge. The blocks of wood be-

gan to dance around and I began to dance around with them and sometimes the wood was on top and sometimes I was. One hefty chunk did a nifty little foxtrot along the left side of my rib cage while another practiced the tango with my hip bone. A clownish piece of tamarack went past wearing my hat, and six or seven other chunks were attempting to perform the same trick with my waders and fishing vest. Still, I didn't want to yell out any of the choice phrases blossoming in my head for fear of offending my rescuers. (There is nothing worse than an offended rescuer.) By the time we reached a car ("This is it!" I yelled out.), I felt as though I had spent the day participating in an avalanche.

Some of the minor rescues are only slightly less disastrous. I am perfectly capable of negotiating barb-wire fences on my own, and on occasions—particularly in pastures with resident bulls—have done so with considerable speed. Nevertheless it frequently happens that a complete stranger will be standing next to a fence which I must climb through, and he will insist upon holding up the wire for me. It almost never fails that this kindly chap immediately reveals himself to have either exceptionally bad timing, a perverted sense of humor, or a handgrip slightly weaker than that of a deep-fried prawn.

Then there are the direction-givers. I am convinced that there are people who, upon hearing that I am trying to find out how to get to Lost Lake, would climb out of an oxygen tent and run barefooted three miles through the snow for the opportunity of giving me directions to it. Now I would appreciate this sacrifice on their part except for one thing: not only have they never been to Lost Lake in their lives, they didn't even know it existed until they heard I wanted to go there. But I shouldn't be too harsh on these people. Even though I don't find Lost Lake by following their directions I do discover some truly great swamps, vast stretches of country distinguished by a total absence of water, campsites with rock-to-rock rattlesnakes, and sometimes a little mountain valley inhabited only by a family of giant bears, all of whom are suffering from acute irritability.

There are times, of course, when I actually have need of rescue. One of these times occurred last fall on Lake Pend Oreille. Mort Haggard and I had stalled our outboard in the middle of the lake just as we noticed the thin black line of a storm edging toward us. There is only one sensible way to ride out a storm on Lake Pend Oreille and that is astride a barstool in the nearest resort. With this object in mind, we were taking turns flailing away on the pull cord when the damn thing broke. The storm was just about upon us and I got out a can and started bailing as fast as I could. We weren't taking any water over the sides yet, but the bottom of the boat was awash in cold sweat.

There was only one other boat in sight and we hailed it by gesturing with our arms in a fashion that the casual observer might have supposed to be frantic. We also loudly repeated the word "help" at regular intervals of a half second and in a somewhat shrill pitch so as to be heard above the wind.

The two occupants of the other boat responded promptly to these signals, and soon had pulled their rather sleek craft up alongside our rather dumpy one. They were husband and wife, both up in their seventies, lean as lances and deeply tanned. The man was conservatively dressed in bib overalls and his wife wore a long flowery dress. Both of them looked safe enough.

Mort and I immediately made the mistake common to persons being rescued, which is to defer in all matters of logic and common sense to the rescuers, the assumption being that because a person is at this moment displaying a keen sense of goodwill, he is therefore not (a) a madman, (b) an imbecile, or (c) a mugger on vacation. Our rescuers, it turned out, were none of these three. They were something else.

"Can you give us a tow to shore?" I shouted at them.

"Oh not too good," the old man said. "We caught two or three earlier, but they was pretty small."

Mort and I grinned uncomfortably and shot nervous glances at each other and the storm.

"Clifford's a mite hard of hearing," said the woman, whose name, we learned, was Alma. "THEY WANT A TOW TO SHORE!" Alma said to Clifford.

"Fine, fine," Clifford said. "You fellas just grab ahold on the side of our boat and we'll tow you in."

This suggestion did not seem to be one of the ten best ideas I had ever heard.

"Don't you think it would be better to rig up a tow line?" I asked.

"They was all silvers," Clifford said. "But they was small."

Mort and I took another look at the storm and grabbed the side of their boat.

Clifford eased out on the throttle and the two boats began to move. There was a good chop on the water now, and the sky was black. Mort and I clung to the side of the other boat as if it were the brink of an eighty-foot cliff.

Clifford let out on the throttle a bit more, pulling Mort and me over on our sides. We wrapped our legs around the seats and locked our ankles together. Our rib cages began to simulate the action of an accordion in a rock band. Charley horses began to gallop up and down my arms.

Clifford eased out on the throttle a bit more, and Mort began to emit a low, continuous moan, which he politely attempted to disguise as humming. "Hummghh, hummghh," he went.

Clifford eased out on the throttle still a bit more, and the bows of both boats were out of the water. Our fishing lines snapped into the air and trailed out behind us like silver streamers in the wind.

"Hey, Cliff," I yelled through the plume of spray. "How about slowing it down some?"

He smiled down at me. "Yup," he said. "They was all small."

Alma meanwhile had taken a liking to Mort and was attempting to engage him in conversation. She had moved over next to him and was shouting down into his free ear, the one not scrunched into an oarlock.

"Bet you can't guess how long we've lived in these parts, can you, young man?" she asked.

"Yes ma'm," said Mort, always the gentleman. "Hummmgh, hummmgh!"

"You can? How long then?"

"Yes ma'm," Mort said. "Hummmmgh, hummmmgh!"

"We've lived here seventy-odd years now, and let me tell you, we've seen some powerful hard times," Alma said, apparently not realizing that she was seeing one of them right then.

"Yes ma'm," Mort said. "Hummmgh, hummmgh."

We smacked into a huge wave. One moment the other boat was above us, Mort and I holding up there, and the next it was down below, dangling from our aching arms, and all of us still going like sixty. Then the two boats began to go their separate ways. Mort and I wrenched them back together, shouting out a rousing chorus from an old sea chanty frequently sung by sailors as they were being keelhauled.

"Thought we was going to lose you for a minute there," Clifford yelled over at us with a grin.

"Yes ma'm," Mort said. "Hummmmgh, hummmmgh!"

When we were once again standing safely on the dock, which didn't seem like a day over three weeks, Mort turned philosophical about the whole adventure. "Look at it this way," he said. "First of all, we probably never would have survived that storm if we hadn't been rescued. Second, we're standing here on the dock soaking our hands in the lake, and we don't even have to bother to bend down."

"Hummgh, hummgh," I said.

"I'll Never Forget Old 5789-A"

LET ME ADMIT it right off. There was a time not too long ago when I liked my wildlife unadorned. What I mean is, I liked it in the naked. Stark raving raw. In its birthday suit. Nude. Stripped. Bare. Some fur or hair and maybe a set of horns, but otherwise unadorned with so much as an aluminum fig leaf.

The wildlife situation, as I saw it, was becoming grim—sciencewise. The scientists were running all over the place decorating my wild animals with vinyl tags, collars, streamers, flags, patches and jackets. They were putting radio transmitters on grizzly bears and sage grouse and sea turtles. Deer in Idaho were running around in blinking lights, and some falcons of my acquaintance carried so much electronic equipment they had to taxi for a take off. So help me, I even knew a mountain goat that ran around for a year with a piece of garden hose on his horns!

And that's not all. Plans were under way, the wildlife scientists told me, to start using telemetry, the system used by NASA doctors to keep tabs on the physiology of astronauts orbiting the globe. That way the zoologists and wildlife managers would know not only the location of a particular animal day and night but his temperature, rate of respiration, heart beat, and no doubt his politics.

All this I found depressing. Whoever expected wildlife managers to actually start managing the wildlife? I personally did not like scientists and the like fooling around with the fauna.

Then one day I said to myself, "You're a modern American male, aren't you? Yes. Therefore you are regimented, inoculated, tranquilized, numbered, recorded, transported, transplanted, poked, probed, polled, conditioned, and computerized, aren't you? Yes. Then," I said to myself, "why should a bunch of damn animals be better off than you are?"

After that I decided to get into the spirit of the thing. The time would come, I saw, when people would think that anyone showing a preference for naked animals must be some kind of pervert. Mothers would call their children off the streets whenever "Fruity Fred" walked by. Toughs would beat him up in bars, and he would have to move to a city where the police protected people like him. He would have to get his kicks by watching clandestine showings of old Disney nature films in motel rooms and maybe even by exchanging pictures of naked deer and bear with persons of similar inclinations. Maybe he would be forced to make his living by peddling picture postcards from an alley: "Wanta buy a dirty picture of a moose?"

None of that was for me. I got scared and started thinking of all the advantages this new scientific approach to game management would bring about. It took a while, but I finally thought of some.

For example, I wouldn't have to slog around in

the woods anymore hunting aimlessly for a deer. I would just stop by the local Electronic Game Control Center.

"What do you have in the way of a nice 125-pound whitetail buck at about 4:15 P.M. in the Haversteads' meadow" I would ask the technologist in charge.

"One moment, please." She would put the last touch to a phony eyelash and then program a card and run it through the computer. *Blink. Buzz. Hummm. Clink!* "You're in luck," she would say, looking at a piece of computer tape. "Buck Deer No. 5789-A will be crossing the Haversteads' meadow at exactly 4:32 P.M. He will be traveling due north at a speed of six miles per hour. His present weight is 135 pounds; pulse rate, 78; and temperature, 99.1. He has had all of his shots."

"Just what I'm looking for," I say, and rush out the door, heading for the Haversteads' meadow.

At precisely 4:32 P.M. Buck Deer No. 5789-A steps into the clearing, heading due north at a speed of six miles per hour. He is wearing a bright red vinyl jacket set off by blue ear streamers and a collar of blinking lights. I bust him with a .30-30 slug, which enters just slightly above his portable power pack and emerges to the left of his transistorized radio unit.

As I rush up to the fallen No. 5789-A, a feminine voice squawks from his radio pack, "Nice shot!" The voice belongs to the lady technologist at the Electronic Game Control Center.

"Thanks," I say.

"I will now put on a recording of the proper method for dressing a big-game animal," she says. Another female voice comes on:

"You have just shot what is known as your big-game animal. Here are the directions for dressing your big-game animal. First carefully remove from the big-game animal all electronic devices, its vinyl jacket and ribbons, and the collar of blinking lights. If this is not done immediately, the meat may have a strong flavor. Step Number Two ..."

You can see the advantages.

The drawbacks, of course, would be minor. For one thing, we would have to add some new terminology. Hunting conversations then might go something like this:

"Heard you gotcher deer."

"Yeah, I busted old 5789-A."

"No kidding! How many transistors did the old boy have?"

"Four. And big! Why that devil was wearing a thirty-eight-inch collar, a size sixty-four jacket, and the biggest whip antenna I ever saw."

There might also be a few additional difficulties in the eating of game. Your wife might have to warn the children, "Be careful you don't crack your teeth on a piece of Daddy's buckshot and watch out for the little wires and electrodes; they might catch in your throat and choke you."

Nevertheless, any extra dental and doctor bills would be more than made up for by your savings on hunting clothes. Since all the animals will be wearing red, the hunters can wear any old thing they want—as long as it isn't red. Wearing red, in fact, might be disastrous. Hunters who mistake people for potential venison will plead, "I saw this flash of red and thought sure it was a deer. . . ."

Now I'm not one to swim upstream in the river of progress. The old days are gone. But I know that sooner or later I'll have a relapse and be carted off to a psychiatrist to be set right.

"What seems to be your problem?" the psychiatrist will ask.

"Well, Doc," I'll say, "I keep thinking about these naked animals."

"Yes," he'll say, "that is rather serious. Such tendencies are doubtlessly the manifestation of some childhood experience."

And you know, he'll be right.

The B'ar

RANCID CRABTREE was ranting and raving when he charged into our kitchen. "Thar's a gol-dang b'ar in maw brush pile," he said.

My grandmother's nose quivered. "Open the window, child," she said to me. Personally, I thought Rancid had a rather interesting smell, kind of tangy, like game hung a bit too long in warm weather.

"What's this about a bear?" Gram asked, shoving a couple of fresh-baked cinnamon rolls in front of Rancid and pouring him a cup of coffee.

"Thar's a b'ar in maw brush pile," Rancid repeated. "Ah thank the critter plans on passin' the winter thar."

"Well, what's that hurt?" Gram said.

Rancid looked at her in disgust. "You can't never tell whan ah might need thet brush pile fer somethin'," he said. "What right's thet b'ar got movin' in like he owned the place? Any number of nice caves around but he's got to hole up in maw brush pile. Wall, ah ain't gonna stand fer it. B'sides, ah've been hungerin' fer some b'ar steak, anyway."

"Then just shoot him and be done with it," Gram said.

"That's what ah needs the boy fer."

"What?" Gram said.

"What?" I said.

"Ah needs him to stand on top the brush pile and poke a pole down into it and drive the b'ar out so ah kin get a shot. Won't be nothin' to it."

"There won't be nothin' to it, all right," Gram said, "because I ain't lettin' him do a fool dangerous thing like that."

Gram and I agreed on few things, but this happened to be one of them. Just to make it look good though, I threw out a half-hearted beg.

"Aw c'mon, Gram, let me do it," I said.

"Nope!"

"All right." There was no point in pushing her too hard.

"What's the matter?" Rancid said, giving me his mean look. "Yer begger broke?"

I could see he was disappointed.

"Hey," I said. "How about Ginger Ann? I bet she'd do it." Ginger Ann was a woman who lived alone back in the hills on a little ranch she had inherited from her father. I'd heard it said of her that she could out-work, out-fight, and out-swear any man in the county. Once I'd seen her ornery old cow horse throw her flat on her back, for no reason that I could see except he thought it might be a good joke. She was up in a flash, fists doubled and biceps knotted up to the size of grapefruit. She delivered the beast such a blow to the ribs he would have fallen over sideways except for a nearby tree. While he was still dazed she stepped back into the saddle and said to me, "Don't mind us, boy. We do this all the time."

That was one of the reasons I thought Ginger Ann might be just the person to drive a bear out of a brush pile.

"Gol-dang," Rancid said, "ah never thought of Ginger Ann. Ah bet she would do it."

"I wouldn't mind going along to watch," I said.

"Suit yerself," Rancid said.

"You just take care you don't get hurt," Gram warned.

"Shucks, thet b'ar ain't gonna hurt nobody," Rancid said.

"It ain't the bear I'm worried about," Gram said.

We got into Rancid's old truck and rattled over to Ginger Ann's place, an ancient log house slouched among a scattering of pine trees and the assorted remains of hay wagons, cars, trucks, tractors, and contraptions that defied identification. She seemed delighted to see us.

"Ah was wonderin' if you would help me to shoot a b'ar," Rancid said to her.

"You bet," Ginger Ann said, taking her .30-30 off the wall. "Let's go."

"Hold on a minute," Rancid said. "You won't be needin' thet thang, because ah'm gonna do the shootin' mawsef. All ah needs you fer is to drive the b'ar out of maw brush pile."

Ginger Ann shoved a box of shells in her jacket pocket. "Why can't you drive the bear out and let me shoot it?"

"Ha!" Rancid said. " 'Cause yer jist a woman, thet's why. Ah never know'd a woman yet could shoot worth a dang."

Ginger Ann stepped out on the porch and pointed to an old car door leaning against a tree thirty yards away. "You see that itty-bitty patch of rust just to the left of the top hinge?" She jacked a shell into the chamber, put the rifle to her shoulder and fired. The door jumped. (There was some question later about whether the door actually jumped, but I saw it.) We walked over, and there was a single bullet hole in the door, drilled neatly through the rust patch.

"Wall anyway," Rancid said, "a car door ain't no b'ar, and ah git to do the shootin' and thet's all thar is to it."

"I'll arm wrestle you then," Ginger Ann said. "Winner shoots the bear."

Rancid sneaked a glance at her right arm. "Ah ain't arm wrastlin' no woman."

They argued and yelled at each other all the time we were driving back to Rancid's place, but finally Ginger gave in and said, yes, she'd drive the bear out of the brush pile.

"All this fightin' has set me on edge," Rancid said. "Let's go in maw cabin and ah'll bile us up a pot of coffee. Than we'll go git the b'ar."

Ginger Ann looked around the cabin while Rancid was blowing dust out of a couple of extra cups and putting the coffee on. "Why don't you ever clean this place up?" she said.

"Gol-dang, what are you talkin' about, woman!" Rancid said, his feelings obviously hurt. "Ah jist cleaned it up!"

"When?"

"Wall, let's see, what month is it now? Anyway, not too long ago."

While we were drinking our coffee Rancid laid out his plan for us. He drew a circle with his finger in the dust on the table. Inside the circle he put a dot. "This hyar's the brush pile," he said, indicating the circle.

"And this is the bear, I suppose," Ginger Ann said, pointing to the dot.

"Nope," Rancid said. "Thet's you, standing on top the brush pile. Directly underneath you is the b'ar."

"Oh," Ginger Ann said.

Rancid drew a little X six inches out from the circle. "This hyar is me." Then he made a dotted line from the dot in the circle halfway out to the X. "This is the b'ar comin' out of the brush pile. Ah'll shoot it right thar."

Ginger Ann reached forward with her finger and very quickly extended the dotted line out to the X and made a violent swirling motion that sent a little puff of dust into the air.

"What you go an' do thet fer?" Rancid said.

"That's what will happen if you miss the bear," Ginger Ann said with a laugh that rattled the stovepipe.

"Ha!" Rancid said. "Ah don't miss!" He looked down at the spot where the little X had been erased. "On t'other hand, ah can probably git a better shot if ah stand over hyar." And he drew another X some distance off to one side.

"Where's Pat going to stand?" Ginger Ann asked.

"There ain't enough room on the table to show that," I said.

When we had finished the coffee, Rancid put on his dirty red hunting shirt ("maw lucky shart"), picked up his ancient .30-30, and we headed out to the brush pile. Ginger Ann carried the pole over her shoulder. The brush pile was in the middle of a small clearing Rancid had cut in the woods when he was a young man and thinking of becoming a farmer. This evidence of ambition embarrassed him considerably, and he explained it away by saying, "Aw was insane at the time."

"Smell thet b'ar smell?" Rancid whispered when we got to the clearing.

"No," Ginger Ann whispered. "All I can smell is . . . When was the last time you took a bath, anyway, Rancid?"

"What y'ar is it now?" Rancid said.

The brush pile was about eight feet high and laced with small logs sticking out at every angle. On one side of it was what appeared to be an opening—the place where Rancid had indicated the bear would exit. After sizing up the situation and making a number of calculations based upon previous experiences I'd had with Rancid, I selected a moderately tall tamarack tree and climbed about halfway up it. My perch on a stout limb gave me a good view of the scene.

Rancid took up his position off to one side of what he had determined to be the bear's path of escape. He seemed a bit nervous. I could see him rummaging around in his pockets, looking for something. Then he took out a plug of tobacco and took a great chaw out of it. He limbered up his arms, and threw the rifle up onto his shoulder a couple of times for practice. All this time Ginger Ann stood leaning on the pole, watching him and shaking her head as if she couldn't believe it all. Finally, Rancid motioned her to climb up on top of the brush pile, and he went into a half crouch, rifle at the ready.

Ginger Ann made such a commotion climbing up the brush pile that I decided there wasn't a bear in there anyway, either that or he was dead or stone deaf. When she was at last on top of the brush pile, she poked several times down into it with the pole. Nothing happened. I could see that Rancid was getting exasperated.

"Gol-dang it, woman," he finally shouted, "jam thet pole down *hard!*"

"If you know so much about it, you knot-headed ignoramus, why don't you come do it yourself," Ginger Ann shouted back.

"Ah shoulda know'd better'n to brang a woman to do a boy's job," Rancid said. "Let me show you how to do it." He leaned his rifle against a tree and started for the brush pile.

By now Ginger Ann's face was red from rage. She lifted the pole above her head and drove it with all her might into the brush.

I didn't see all that happened next because I blinked. The bear didn't bother using the door to the brush pile but just crashed out through the side of it—the side toward Rancid. The brush pile seemed to explode, and Ginger Ann toppled over backwards, screaming, "Shoot, Rancid, shoot—before it's too late!"

Well, it was about the most exciting and interesting spectacle I've ever had the good fortune to witness for free. I saw Rancid turn and run, and I thought he was going for the rifle, but he went right past without even giving it a glance. Right then was when I blinked. When the blink was over, the bear was just a black streak twenty yards away. A few feet ahead of the black streak was a dirty red streak. Rancid's hat was still suspended in the air where he had been standing when the bear first came out of the brush pile. Ginger Ann finally hit the ground, still screaming,

"Shoot! Shoot!" Off in the distance I could see the black streak and the red streak going up a hill. About halfway up the hill, the black streak passed the red streak, but Rancid was apparently so intent on making a good showing, he didn't even notice. Or maybe he was running with his eyes shut. In any case, when they went over the hill, Rancid was still running hard and looked as if he might be gaining on the bear.

I slid down out of the tree, and Ginger Ann ran around the brush pile and grabbed Rancid's rifle.

"Are you going after them?" I asked.

"No," she said. "If they run by here again, maybe I'll shoot the bear for Rancid. Then again, maybe I won't."

After about twenty minutes, a bedraggled Rancid came shuffling back to the clearing. Without saying a word, he took his rifle out of Ginger Ann's hand and headed for the cabin. Ginger Ann and I trailed along behind.

"No point in feeling bad about it," Ginger Ann said after a bit. "It could have happened to anybody."

"Ah had maw mouth all set fer some b'ar steak," Rancid said, glumly. "Ah guess ah should have let you do the shootin'."

"Shucks," Ginger Ann said. "I couldn't even hit an old car door. You know that bullet hole in the rust spot? Why, that's been in there ever since my daddy shot it in there years ago."

"Ha!" Rancid said, brightening up. "Ah know'd thet."

"But . . ." I said.

"C'mon in the cabin," Rancid said to Ginger Ann, "and I'll bile us up another pot of coffee."

"Don't mind if I do," she said.

"But, Rancid . . ." I said.

"See you later," Ginger Ann said to me. She shoved Rancid into the cabin and shut the door before I could warn him.

I couldn't understand it. Here Ginger Ann had made one of the finest shots I had ever seen, and then she turned right around and lied about it. She had to be up to something, but I didn't know what, and it worried me. Before going home, I yelled at the top of my voice, "I saw the car door jump when she shot, Rancid! I saw it jump!"

He didn't seem to hear me.

The
Rendezvous

EVERY HUNTER KNOWS what a rendezvous is. That's where one hunter says to another, "Al, you take that side of the draw and I'll take this one and we'll meet in twenty minutes at the top of the hill." The next time they see each other is at a PTA meeting five years later in Pocatello. That's a rendezvous.

It is simply against the basic nature of hunters to arrive at a designated point at a designated time. If one of my hunting pals said, "I'll meet you on the other side of this tree in ten seconds," one of us would be an hour late. And have the wrong tree besides.

We work out complicated whistling codes as a means of staying in touch. "One long and two shorts means I've found some fresh sign and for the other guy to come on over. Two shorts and one long mean . . ." etc. I go no more than fifteen feet and stumble onto the tracks of a herd of mule deer. They are so fresh the earth is still crumbling from the edges. I whistle the code, low and soft. No answer. I try again, louder. No answer. Then I cut loose with a real blast. Still no answer. By now I've forgotten all about the deer, and whistle so loud the crew at a sawmill three miles away go off shift an hour early. My upper lip has a charley horse and I think I have a slight hernia. The only way he could have gotten out of hearing so fast was if he had a motorcycle hidden behind a bush.

Some hunters have even resorted to two-way radios, but to little avail. "Charley One, this is Hank Four. Come in Charley One." Charley One doesn't come in. All you can get is some guy in Australia. He is saying, "Roger, I'm onto the bloody biggest tracks you ever saw. Roger? Where the 'ell are you, Roger?"

Why is it so difficult to keep a rendezvous? Usually it is because both hunters are not familiar with the terrain being hunted. But one thinks he is. He is the one who lays out the strategy.

A couple of years ago a friend and I were hunting near the Washington-Canadian border in country so rough it looks like it was whipped up in the lava stage by a giant egg beater and left to dry. The mountains do not have ranges like decent mountains: they have convulsions.

"You cut down over the side of the mountain," my friend said casually, "and I'll swing around with the car and pick you up on the road."

"You sure there's a road down there?" I asked.

"Of course," he said. "You'll come to a little stream and the road is just on the other side of it. There's no way in the world you can miss it."

True to the nature of rendezvous, there was at least one way in the world to miss it. Six hours later, after having scaled down cliffs that would have made a mockery of the precipices in alpine movies, I came to a stream. By my reckoning, it should have been running from my right to left; instead it was running from left to right. There was no sign of a road on the other side. I sat down calmly to take stock of the situation. When that proved too frightening, I leaped up, plunged into the stream, and started climbing the nearest mountain.

The thought that I might starve to death before getting out of that wilderness occurred to me, and I promptly shot the head off a grouse at about forty yards (a feat that prior to and after that moment has always eluded me), plucked it, dressed it, and stowed it away in the game pocket of my hunting jacket. Squads of deer, like characters out of some Disney film, gazed upon me from all sides, no doubt wondering what kind of strange creature this was crashing frantically through their forest primeval. They went ignored, except when I had to drive them out of my way with shrill and vulgar shouts.

Eventually I came to a road and flagged down a car by lying down in front of it. I was relieved to discover that the hunters in it spoke English and that I was still on American soil. An hour later I was seated at a roadhouse downing the first course of what I intended to be a ten-course meal, when my hunting partner burst through the door and started calling for volunteers for a search party.

"Who's lost?" I asked.

"You!" he cried. And then he uttered those words invariably uttered at the resolution of ill-fated rendezvous: "What the ———— happened to you? I waited . . ."

Such was the traumatic nature of my ordeal that I forgot all about the grouse I had shot. Late that night my wife was cleaning out my hunting jacket and thrust her hand into the game pocket to find out what that peculiar bulge was. The resulting scream sent half the people on our block into the street.

"What," my shaking spouse asked me as I came back in from the street, "is that bird doing in there?"

"That," I growled, "was provisions, in case I had to spend the winter in those ———— mountains."

One of the axioms of hunting is that more time is spent hunting for hunting companions than for deer. I always feel that a hunt is successful if just one rendezvous is completed. Whether or not we get any deer is incidental:

"How was your hunting trip?"

"Wonderful! We met where and when we were supposed to one out of nine times."

"Get any deer?"

"Didn't see a thing."

When I was a high school kid I used to hunt with an old man who had truly mastered the art of the rendezvous. He always directed the hunt, which may have been part of his secret.

"You cut down through that brush there, work your way around the side of the mountain, climb up to the ridge, and circle back to the truck. I'll do likewise on the other side, and we'll meet back here in an hour."

"That's impossible," I would say.

"Listen, if an old man like me can do it, you can."

Two hours later I would stagger in, scratched, bruised and torn, and there the Old Man would be, fresh as a daisy, sitting on the tailgate of the truck drinking coffee out of my thermos. More often than not he would have a deer.

"What took you so long?" he would say.

The uncanny thing about the Old Man was that

no matter when you got back to the truck, even if it was just fifteen minutes after leaving, he would somehow sense your return and with some superhuman effort manage to get back and be waiting for you. But he was always modest about his talent, this sixth sense for keeping a rendezvous.

"It's nothing, boy," he would say. "It's just a little somethin' that comes to you with old age."

Cigars, Logging Trucks, and Know-It-Alls

A WHILE BACK I was asked what I thought were the three greatest threats to a fisherman's well-being. Although this is not a question one hears every day, I have over the years given the subject much thought and was able to answer immediately: "Cigars, logging trucks, and know-it-alls."

My interrogator was somewhat taken aback by this reply, obviously having expected a listing of such standard dangers as bears, bulls, rattlesnakes, rapids, quicksand, dropoffs, etc. Although these are all very real dangers and may frequently threaten premature termination of one's existence, the whole bunch of them together does not equal the potential for destruction compressed into a single small cigar, let alone a logging truck or a know-it-all.

Twice in the past year alone I have been witness to two unwarranted and unprovoked attacks by a cigar upon innocent anglers. In the first instance the cigar, a small sporty El Puffo, nearly wiped out three fishermen, a dog, and a 1958 pickup truck. It happened like this:

My friends Herb and Retch and I and Herb's dog, Rupert, had spent the day fishing a high mountain lake and were headed home, the four of us crowded in the cab, by way of a road that traverses the edge of a one-thousand-foot-deep gorge named, appropriately, Deadman's. Herb usually smokes a pipe, but since he had run out of tobacco Retch had offered him a plastic-tipped cigar. Chewing nervously on the cigar, Herb pampered the pickup along the road, the outer wheels nudging rocks into thin air. The silence was broken only by the sound of dripping sweat, an occasional inhalation or exhalation, and the dog Rupert popping his knuckles. Then it happened. Forgetting he was smoking a cigar, Herb reached up in the manner of removing a pipe from his mouth and closed his hand over the glowing tip of the El Puffo.

"*Ahhhhaaaiiigh!*" Herb said, grinding his foot down on the gas pedal.

"*Ahhhhaaaiiigh!*" the rest of us said. In an instant six hands and two paws were clamped on the steering wheel. Retch claimed later that he jumped out twice but both times the pickup was so far out in space he had to jump back in. In any case there was about as much activity in that pickup cab as I have ever witnessed before in such cramped quarters. When it was all over and we were safe again, I was driving, Herb and Retch were crouched on the floor, and the dog was smoking the cigar.

Then there was the time down on the Grande Ronde River when Retch was so startled by a nine-pound steelhead hitting his lure that a lighted cigar stub popped out of his mouth and dropped inside the open top of his waders. Naturally a man doesn't turn loose of a nine-pound steelhead just because he has a lighted cigar roaming around inside his waders. He just makes every effort to keep the cigar in constant motion and, if possible, away from any areas particularly susceptible to fire-and-smoke damage.

Retch knew all this, of course, and managed to land the steelhead in record time. Although his injuries from the cigar were only minor I thought possibly some of the other fishermen nearby might bring charges against him. First, there was his use of vile language, but since it was screeched at such a high pitch as to be understood only by members of the canine family and lip-readers who had served at least one hitch in the Marine Corps, I thought it unlikely that much of a case could be made on that count. On the other hand, there was a good chance he might have been convicted of obscene dancing on a trout stream. And finally there was the felonious act of attempting to induce innocent bystanders to laugh themselves to death.

Cigars are dangerous enough, but logging trucks are a good deal worse. Some younger readers, particularly those living in the plains states, may not be familiar with logging trucks, so here is a brief description: the natural habitat of logging trucks is steep, winding, narrow roads situated between high mountain trout streams and the state highway. Where I live, in the Pacific Northwest, they are a protected species. They weigh several tons and are in the habit of hauling sections of large trees around on their backs. No one knows why, unless they eat them. The term "logging trucks" is their scientific name; fishermen, however, commonly refer to them as blankety-blank-of-a-blank, as in "Great gosh-a-mighty, Harry, here comes a blankety-blank-of-a-blank!"

Logging trucks are almost always encountered

at the end of a steep, winding stretch of narrow road where the only turnouts are three miles behind your vehicle and ten feet behind the logging truck. To those inexperienced in such matters, the fair and reasonable course of action might seem to be that the logging truck would back up the ten feet to the turnout and let you pass, but that is not the way it works. The rules are that you must back up the three miles, usually at speeds in excess of 30 mph, while your passengers shout such words of encouragement as, "Watch that washout!" and "Faster! The blankety-blank-of-a-blank is gaining on us!"

Several years ago I made it to the turnout at the top of a mountain road just as a logging truck, its timing slightly off, was pulling up for its winding descent of the mountain road, no doubt intending to drive before it a car full of hapless, shouting, fist-shaking fishermen. The logging truck pulled abreast of my car, spat a chaw of tobacco out the window and said, "Shucks, that don't happen very often." I could see the logging truck was disappointed at not catching me ten feet short of the turnout but that was its tough luck.

Most of my friends and I have become excellent logging truck trackers over the years. You track a logging truck about the same way you track a deer. You get out and look for signs. The droppings from a logging truck consist of branches and twigs from its load of logs and occasionally the front bumper from a late model sedan. Any road with such signs scattered along it may be regarded as a game trail for logging trucks.

Occasionally there are other signs to be read. They say, DANGER—LOGGING TRUCKS. These signs are usually put up by other fishermen in the hope of keeping a good piece of fishing water to themselves. This is a despicable trick, since an angler can ignore such signs only at his peril. As with any other dedicated angler, I am not above putting fresh grizzly claw marks nine feet high on a pine tree alongside a trail to a good mountain lake. But I would never stoop to putting up a logging truck warning sign. That's going a little bit too far.

Know-it-alls are by far the greatest threat to the well-being of the angler. Your average run-of-the-mill know-it-all can reduce a fisherman to a quivering, babbling wreck with nothing more than a few well-chosen pieces of advice.

Know-it-alls are sometimes difficult to spot since they come in all sizes, shapes, and sexes. They are all equally dangerous. A trembling little old lady know-it-all can be as lethal as a three-hundred-pound madman with an ax in either hand. Their one distinguishing characteristic is a self-confidence as total as it is sublime.

Know-it-alls have probably gotten me in more trouble than all the other dangers put together. I recall one time a know-it-all and I were out fishing and decided to hunt for wild mushrooms. We drove up to a grassy meadow and I suggested that we leave the pickup on high ground and walk across the meadow because it looked wet to me.

"Naw, it ain't wet," the know-it-all said. "You can drive across."

So I steered the pickup down into the high grass of the meadow. After a bit the wheels started to slip in mud.

"Hey, it's getting wet," I said. "We better turn back."

"Naw. It's just a little damp here. You can make it across."

Then plumes of water started spraying out on both sides of the car.

"You better speed up a bit going through this puddle," the know-it-all said.

I speeded up. Pretty soon we were plowing up a sizable wake.

"Pour on the gas!" shouted the know-it-all. "We're nearly to the other side of the puddle."

By now I was in a cold sweat. The pickup was bouncing, sliding, and twisting through the high grass and waves of water were crashing across the windshield. Suddenly, the grass parted ahead of us and we shot out into a bright clear expanse of open water.

Later, dripping with mud and wrath, I paid off the tow truck man back at his gas station.

One of the hangers-on at the station finally put down his bottle of pop and asked, "How come y'all got so muddy?"

"Drove his pickup out into the middle of Grass Lake," the tow truck man said.

"Oh," the other man said.

Here are some statements that immediately identify the know-it-all:

"Hell, that ain't no bull, Charley, and anyway you could outrun it, even if your waders are half full of water."

"Quicksand? That ain't quicksand! You think I don't know my quicksand? Now git on in there and wade across."

"Course it feels hot. That's a sign they're beginning to dry. See how the steam is risin' off 'em? Now you just keep holding your feet over the fire like that till your boots are good and dry."

"Ain't no rattlesnakes in these parts."

"Ain't no logging trucks in these parts."

"You ever eat any of these little white berries? Taste just like wild hickory nuts."

"With thin ice what you have to do is just walk real fast so it don't have time to break under you. Now git on out there and let's see how fast you can walk. Faster! Faster! Dang it, didn't I tell you to walk fast?"

Because of such advice, the know-it-all is now listed as a threatened species. I myself have threatened a large number of them and, on occasion, have even endangered a few.

But Where's the Park, Papa?

ON ONE OF THE DOGGIER of last summer's dog days, my family and I simmered grimly in our own juices as we toiled along, a bit of the flotsam in a sluggish river of traffic. Our rate of speed was somewhere between a creep and an ooze. Heat waves pulsed in a blue sea of exhaust fumes. Blood boiled and nerves twitched. Red-faced, sweating policemen would occasionally appear and gesture angrily at the drivers to speed it up or slow it down. At least one of the drivers felt like gesturing back.

We were on one of those self-imposed exiles from the amenities of civilized life popularly referred to as vacations. I was in my usual vacation mood, which is something less than festive. My kids were diligently attempting to perfect the art of whining, while my mother expressed her growing concern and disbelief at the sparcity of restrooms along this particular stretch of highway. Whenever the speed of the traffic slowed to the ooze stage, my wife took the opportunity to spoon tranquilizers into my mouth from a cereal bowl, all the while urging me not to enlarge the children's vocabulary too far beyond their years. Mother, in her increasing anxiety, already had them up to about age forty-seven.

"Hey," one of the kids paused in mid-whine to complain. "You said you was gonna take us to a national park!"

"Clam up!" I counseled him, drawing upon my vast store of child psychology. "This *is* a national park!"

To keep the children amused until we found a park campsite, my wife invented one of those games which start with the idea of increasing the youngsters' awareness of their environment and end with them beating each other with tire irons in the back seat. As I recall, this particular game resulted in a final score of three, six, and eight points. Each kid got one point for every square foot of ground he spotted first that didn't have any litter on it.

I can recall a time when tourists visiting national parks appeared to be folks indulging themselves in a bit of wholesome outdoor enjoyment. Now they seem to have a sense of desperation about them, like people who have fled their homes nine minutes before the arrival of Genghis Khan. Most of them no longer have any hope of seeing unspoiled wilderness, but they have heard rumors that the parks are places where the ground is still unpaved. Of course, if they want to see this ground they have to ask the crowd of people standing on it to jump into the air in unison.

The individuals I really feel sorry for are the serious practitioners of littering. Some of these poor souls have hauled their litter a thousands miles or more under the impression they would have the opportunity

of tossing it out into a pristine wilderness, only to discover that they have been preceded by a vast multitude
of casual wrapper-droppers. (The Park Service does
make a heroic effort to keep the litter cleared from
along the highways but is handicapped because its rotary
plows don't work well on paper and beverage bottles.)

Since there are many people who get the bends
and have to be put into decompression chambers if they
get more than thirty minutes from a shopping center,
the parks, at least the one we were in, provide the usual
cluster of supermarkets and variety stores. Here it was
possible to buy plastic animals at a price that suggested
they were driven on the hoof all the way from Hong
Kong. I refused to buy my youngsters any of these
souvenirs. I told them they should find something that
was truly representative of the park, and they did. Each
of them picked up and brought home a really nice piece
of litter.

I find the rangers to be about the most enjoy-
able thing in national parks anymore. I always make a
point to take my children by the ranger station to watch
the rangers climb the walls. In recent years the rangers
have been going on R and R in such places as New York
and Los Angeles in order to get away from the crowds
and noise and to get a breath of fresh air. By the end of
the peak season they have facial twitches so bad they
have to wear neck braces to guard against whiplash.

The park bears aren't what they used to be
either. Most of the bears you see along the roads look
as if they've spent the past five years squatted in a chair
before a television set drinking beer and eating corn
chips. Half of them should be in intensive care units.
They have forgotten what it is that a bear is supposed
to do. If panhandling along the roads were outlawed,
they would probably hustle pool for a living. A dose of

pure air would drop them like a shot through the heart from a .44 Magnum. Any bear that wanders more than a mile from the road has to carry a scuba tank on his back filled with carbon monoxide. As far as spectacle goes, the bears just don't have it anymore. I'd rather drive my kids across town to watch their uncle Harry nurse a hangover. Now there's a spectacle!

Camping in a national park is an invigorating experience. My seventy-year-old mother went off looking for a restroom among the sea of tents, cabins, and campers. After about an hour of unsuccessful searching, she was loping along looking for a path that led off into the wilderness and came upon a wild-eyed man loping in the opposite direction.

"Sir," she said as they passed, "could you tell me where I can find a restroom?"

"I don't know, lady," he shouted over his shoulder. "I've been here for three days and haven't found one yet!"

Some parks still have excellent fishing in them if you can find it, but on the easily accessible streams you would have better luck digging for clams in Montana. There are of course the tame fish planted by the park service, and these can be caught with a bent pin on the end of a clothesline with bubble gum for bait. The sight of a live insect or even a dry fly makes them nauseous. Catching one of them is almost as exciting as changing the water in the goldfish bowl. After being dumped into one of the park streams the fish quickly adjust to their new environment, however, and within a week or two are consuming vast quantities of soggy hot dog buns and cigarette butts. (Scientists estimate that eating one of these fish is equivalent to eating two loaves of bread and four packs of cigarettes.) If anti-littering eventually catches on, a lot of fish will be up

alongside the highways with the bears. They'll be beg-
ging smokes from tourists.

Many people are under the mistaken impression that
transistor radios come from Japan, but that is not the
case. Transistor radios breed in national parks and from
there move out to infest the rest of the country. Their
mating cries at night are among the most hideous
sounds on earth, approximately on the order of those of
catamounts with arthritis. The offspring are prodigious
in number. During the day you can see hundreds of
youngsters carrying the baby transistor radios around
the park. I proposed to a park ranger that a season be
opened on the adults of the species with an eye to limiting the population growth. He said he himself was all
for it but that park regulations forbid hunting of any
kind.

The site on which we finally pitched our tent
was in the middle of a vast caldron of writhing humanity. This made it easy to meet interesting people. Several times I chatted with the fellow next door about his
hobby of pumping the exhaust from his car into our
tent. The fellows on the other side of us were members
of a rock band. For a long time I thought they were
just pounding dents out of their bus, but it turned out
they were practicing. Their rendition of "A Truck Full
of Empty Milk Cans Crashing into a Burglar Alarm
Factory" was kind of catchy, but the rest of their stuff
was much too loud for my taste. People would also drop
into our tent at all hours. They would look about for a
second or two, a puzzled expression on their faces, then
leave. Then we discovered that the trail to the restroom
passed under our tent. This discovery made Mother
noticeably happy and she vanished like a shot up the
trail.

I decided that the best thing to do was to give up on tenting and try to get into one of the park tourist cabins. After mortgaging our home and indenturing two of the children for fourteen years, we managed to scrape together sufficient rent for two nights. The architecture of the cabin was about halfway between Neoshack and Neolithic. Frank Lloyd Wright would have loved it because it blended so naturally into its surroundings—a superb replica of a hobo jungle.

The only good thing about the cabin was that the roof didn't leak all the time we were there. Of course if it had rained, there's no telling what might have happened. It is doubtful that the seine net used for roofing would have kept us dry, but I figured we could always set up the tent inside the cabin.

Our days at the park were filled with the delights of viewing the marvelous phenomena. There was the spring hot enough to boil an egg in, and someone was running a scientific experiment to see if it would do the same thing for an old newspaper and a half-eaten hamburger. Reflection Lake was truly beautiful, with the scraggly spruce trees around its edges so sharply defined in the glass on the lake bottom that you could make out the hatchet marks on them. The Painted Rocks were interesting in their own way, especially where park employees had managed to remove some of the paint. The kids seemed to enjoy the ancient hieroglyphics to be found everywhere: "Fred & Edith Jones, Peanut Grove, Calif.—1968," etc. Then there were the antics of the wildlife. Once we were fortunate enough to observe two mature male Homo sapiens locking horns in a territorial dispute over a parking spot.

Just when I finally found a way to amuse myself in the park, my wife insisted that we leave. She was afraid I would get arrested for trying to poach transistor radios with rocks. Also, while attempting to photograph a bald woodpecker, she flushed a covey of young people deeply engrossed in their own particular study of nature. (If the truth were known, she was probably more flushed than they.) Anyway, she said the only vistas she wanted to see for some time to come were the insides of the four walls of our mortgaged house. We hit the road for home the next day.

Next summer I think I'll skip the national parks and take my family to a place I know up in the Rockies. It doesn't have all the conveniences and accommodations of a national park, of course. The bears aren't especially friendly (but if you do see one, he doesn't look as if he recently escaped from an iron lung). If you have the sudden urge to buy a plastic animal, you just have to grit your teeth and bear it. The scenery isn't all that spectacular, unless you get a little excited over invisible air. The place doesn't have even a geyser, but when I get there it will at least have an old geaser. Some people like to watch him sit on a log and smoke his pipe, in particular a certain middle-aged woman and four ignorant kids. If you need more spectacle than that, you can always go to a national park.

A Yup of a
Different
Color

ABOUT THREE WEEKS before the opening of the first deer season in which I had been guaranteed permission to be an active participant, our resident deer vanished. All that remained of them was some sign sprinkled arrogantly among the plundered rows of our garden. (Since I was only fourteen at the time and not much good at reading deer signs, I could only guess that the message was some complaint about the quality of our cabbage.)

Among the rules that had been laid down by my mother in allowing me to go in armed pursuit of that mythical creature, My First Deer, was one that stated in no uncertain terms that I would have to confine my hunting to our own farm. Somehow the deer had gotten word of this fine print in the contract and immediately (no doubt snickering among themselves) split for the next county.

When I reported this act of treachery to my friend and mentor Rancid Crabtree, the old mountain man offered scant sympathy.

"Why hell, boy, they wouldn't call it deer huntin' if you didn't have to hunt fer the critters," he said. "Shootin' a deer in yer own pea patch ain't huntin', it's revenge."

I explained to Rancid that if a grown, mature man of unsurpassed excellence in the art and science of hunting were to speak firmly to my mother about the importance of shooting one's first deer and to forthwith offer his services as a guide and overseer of such an endeavor, my mother probably would withdraw the stipulation that I hunt exclusively within the boundaries of the farm. Rancid replied that he had a bad headache, his old war wounds were acting up, and he thought he was going blind in one eye, but if he managed to live for a few days longer and just happened to run across such a man he would convey my message to him. We spent the better part of an afternoon sparring about like that until Rancid could stand it no more and finally broke down and invited me to go hunting with him and Mr. Hooker, a tall, stringy old woodsman who lived a mile up the road from our place.

"I don't know what ol' Hook is gonna think about this," Rancid said somewhat morosely. "Me and him ain't never took no kid with us before."

"Well for gosh sakes don't take one along this time," I told him severely. "Just you and me and Mr. Hooker."

"I reckon that'll be more'n enough," Rancid agreed.

I should mention that both my mother and grandmother were harshly critical of Rancid's lifestyle. One time I asked Gram exactly what it was that Rancid Crabtree did for a living.

"He's an idler," she said without hesitation.

I decided right then and there that I wanted to be an idler too, because it gave you so much time off from the job, and I intended at first opportunity to have Rancid teach me the trade. It wasn't until I was thirty years old that I realized he had succeeded at that task.

Although both Mom and Gram disapproved of Rancid's artful striving for an uninterrupted state of leisure, they were secretly fond of the man and even on occasion spoke begrudgingly of his skills as an outdoorsman. As a result, Rancid's halfhearted suggestion that I accompany him and Mr. Hooker on a hunting trip won immediate approval from the family.

The great hunting expedition was set for the middle of the season so I still had plenty of time to sharpen my eye on pheasants, grouse, and ducks and to put in an occasional appearance at school lest the teachers completely forget my name and face.

One of the interesting things about your first deer is that it has a habit of showing up where least expected, even in school. Toward the end of geometry class my deer would occasionally drift in to browse on the isosceles triangles and parallelograms, and once it bounded right through the middle of sophomore English, not only startling me but scaring hell out of Julius Caesar and Brutus.

"Caesar, that deer almost ran you down!" cried Brutus.

"Et tu, Brute?" exclaimed Caesar.

"Whatchername there in the back row," shouted Miss Fitz, the English teacher. "Stop the dreaming and get on with your work!"

It should not be assumed that my days at school were devoid of serious scholarship. Indeed, every morning before classes started I and my cronies would gather in the gymnasium to exchange learned lectures on that aspect of alchemy devoted to turning a set of deer tracks into venison.

These morning gatherings presented an interesting study of the caste system prevalent among young deer hunters. One was either a Yup or a Nope, depending upon his answer to that age-old question, "Gotcher deer yet?" I, of course, was still a Nope.

Although Yups and Nopes looked pretty much alike they were as different as mallards from mongooses. For one thing, a Yup would preface all his lectures with the statement, "I recollect the time I shot my first deer." Now the reason he recollected this historic event so well was that it had probably occurred no further in the past than the previous weekend. The use of the word "first" of course implied that he had downed a good many deer since. Those little nuances in the use of language were the privileges of Yup rank, and none of us Nopes challenged or even begrudged them. We aspired to be Yups someday ourselves. In fact, I wanted to be a Yup so badly I could taste it. And the taste was very sweet indeed.

This caste system was an efficient and humane way of determining the proper social level of a new kid in school. While we were standing in the gym sizing him up on his first morning, somebody would ask, "Gotcher deer yet?"

Depending upon his answer, he would be accepted immediately as a mature, respected member into the community of Yups or relegated to the humble ranks of us unsuccessful Nopes.

If the new kid said "Yup" to the question, his tone would be so modest and matter-of-fact the uninitiated might assume that he was dismissing the topic as unworthy of further consideration. Nothing could be further from the truth. If he was a bona fide Yup, the entire defensive line of the Los Angeles Rams could not have dissuaded him from relating every last detail of that momentous occasion. He would start off with what he had for breakfast on the morning in question, whether he ate one slice of toast or two, whether the toast was burnt, on which side it was burnt, and the degree of the burns. It might be assumed that this toast would eventually play some crucial part in the shooting of the deer, but its only significance was that it was eaten on the morning of that great day. This known power of one's first deer to transform minor details into events of lasting historic significance was the chief test we used to determine the authenticity of Yups.

Announcing the news that you had just changed your status from Nope to Yup was a problem almost as great as getting the first deer. Obviously, you could not rush up to the guys shouting some fool thing like, "I got my first deer! I got my first deer!" The announcement had to be made with oblique casualness, in an offhand manner. The subtle maneuvers employed toward this end included the old standby of wrapping an empty rifle shell in a handkerchief. (Any old empty would do.) When the handkerchief was pulled out, the shell fell to the floor in front of the assembled Yups and Nopes. "Dang, I dropped my lucky shell," the new Yup would say. "Careful you don't step on my lucky shell there, I sure wouldn't want to lose my lucky shell." Only a person with uncommon restraint could keep from asking, "What's so lucky about that shell?" Most of us Nopes, it should be noted, were possessed of uncommon restraint.

Another trick was to wear deer hair on your

pants until someone noticed. Occasionally, you would pick a deer hair off and fling it to the floor, saying loudly, "Dang, I got deer hair all over my pants!" A skilled practitioner of this art could make a handful of hair last most of a week or until everyone within a ten-mile radius had been made aware of his new status as a Yup. Naturally, if during this period his parents or possibly school officials required that he change his pants there was the tedious job of transferring the deer hairs to the new pair.

My hunting trip with Rancid and Mr. Hooker approached with all the speed of a glacier, but I put the time to good use in making preparation. I studied every book and article on hunting in the local library. I even took notes, which I carefully recorded in a loose-leaf notebook. A typical note went something like this: "Deer Horns—Banging two deer horns together is a good way to get deer to come within shooting range. A hunter should always have a couple of deer horns handy."

The notebook contained about four thousand such tips, most of which I forgot immediately upon reading them. For a while I considered carrying this vast reservoir of knowledge along with me for quick reference just in case I should run into my deer up in the mountains and forget what to do.

At long last the great day arrived. Rancid picked me up in his old truck at four in the morning and then we rattled over to Mr. Hooker's place. Mr. Hooker was a fine, hard old gentleman with a temper slightly shorter than a snake's hind legs. I seemed to have a knack for setting off this temper. Mr. Hooker had no more than settled himself on the seat alongside me than he instantly shot up and banged his head on the roof. The string of oaths thus ignited sizzled, popped, and banged for upwards of five minutes.

"What in gosh almighty tarnation dingbat dang is that on the seat?" he roared at me. "It liked to stab me half to death!"

"Just my deer horns," I told him indignantly. "But they seem to be all right. I don't think you hurt them none."

Mr. Hooker said he was mighty relieved to hear that.

Going up into the mountains, everyone's mood improved considerably. Rancid and Mr. Hooker told all the old stories again, starting each one off with "I ever tell you the time . . . ?" And we drank scalding black coffee and ate the fat homemade doughnuts Gram had sent along, and the two men puffed their pipes and threw back their heads and roared with laughter at their own stories, and it was all a fine thing to be doing, going up into the dark, frozen mountains early in the morning with those two old hunters, and I knew that I ᴠanted to do this very same thing forever.

I didn't get my first deer that day or even that first season, but that was all right. Up until then I thought the only reason people went deer hunting was to hunt deer. We were after bigger game than that, I found—game rarer than a four-point unicorn. And bouncing along in Rancid's old truck, squeezed in between those two rough, exotic-smelling, cantankerous old woodsmen, I became a Yup without ever having fired a shot, a kind of Yup that I hadn't even known existed. It never bothered me too much that nobody ever asked that particular question.

Besides, I'd had other kinds of hunting success, and when a new kid arrived in school and I wanted to size him up, I could always ask, "Gotcher duck yet?"

Mountain Goats Never Say "Cheese!"

SOMEWHERE UP AHEAD, beyond the green cleavage of a mountain pass, a Fish and Game helicopter was waiting for me on a wilderness landing strip. I was several hours late for the rendezvous, having been nearly swept into oblivion while fording the river. Then there had been the long climb up to where I now found myself, inching along a game trail that ran perilously close to the edge of the gorge. Far down below, through the lingering tatters of morning fog, I could see water churning among giant boulders. Every few feet I had to stop to catch my breath and wipe the perspiration from my eyes. It wouldn't have been so bad if I had been equipped with decent mountain-climbing gear—rope, ice ax, lug-soled boots—but I was driving my car.

Little would the casual observer of that strange scene have realized that here was a man at the apex of his career as a great outdoor photographer. I didn't realize it myself. Here I thought I was just getting started in the trade but already I was at my apex. Ahead lay defeat, humiliation, poverty. Sadly enough, that was also what lay behind. I have never ceased to marvel at how low some apexes can be.

One of my numerous ambitions as a youngster had been to become a great outdoor photographer. No sooner had a small box camera come into my possession than I was out taking pictures of the outdoors. I remember hauling my first roll of exposed film down to Farley's drugstore to get it developed. I supposed that Mr. Farley did the work himself in the backroom but he said, no, he "farmed it out" to a laboratory in a distant city. The film was gone so long I began to think the distant city must be Nome, the delivery service a lame sloth traveling by snowshoes.

I hounded Mr. Farley daily about the pictures. "Any word from Nome?" I would say. "Any sign of the lame sloth?"

"Patience, my boy, patience," he would reply. Still, I began to sense that he too was awaiting the photos with an expectancy only slightly less urgent than my own.

Finally, a little yellow-and-black envelope with my name on it arrived, and as I pried up the flap with trembling fingers, Mr. Farley leaned forward and peered breathlessly over my shoulder, which was a good way to have Mr. Farley peer over your shoulder; his breath could drive ticks off a badger. I pulled out a perforated string of glossy black-and-white prints and Mr. Farley let out a long sigh of appreciation, scarcely buckling my knees in the excitement of the moment.

"Wow! Look at this!" I said to him.

"Yes, indeed," Mr. Farley said. "Uh, what is it?"

"The outdoors." I told him, trying to conceal my contempt for his lack of perception. "That's what us outdoor photographers take pictures of—the outdoors."

"Oh, yes, I see that now. Some nice gray dirt and gray sky and some nice gray rocks and gray brush. Very nice, particularly if you like gray as much as I do."

We looked at another print.

"That's one of the finest shots of a flyspeck I've ever seen," Mr. Farley said.

I stared at him in disbelief. "That's a chicken hawk!'

"Of course it is. I was just joshin' ya. Over here is the chicken, right?"

"*That,*" I said with controlled rage, "is a *flyspeck!*"

After Mr. Farley mistook four ants on a paper plate for a herd of deer in a snowstorm, I folded up my pictures and went home. Although outdoor photographers are noted for their patience, they can stand only so much.

From then on I spent endless hours out in the woods photographing wildlife. Most of the shots were just your routine beautiful wildlife pictures, but every so often I would get an exceptionally fine photograph which I would honor with a title. There was, for example, "Log Leaped Over by Startled Four-Point Buck One Half-Second Before Shutter Was Snapped." Many people told me the picture was so vivid they could almost see the buck. Another really great shot was "Tip of Tail Feather of Pheasant in Flight." My favorite was "Rings on Water After Trout Jumped."

I took these photographs and others into the editor of our weekly newspaper in the hope he would have the good sense to buy them. He told me he thought I had the instincts of a great outdoor photographer but possibly my reflexes were a bit slow.

The years slipped by almost without my notic-
ing, and one morning I awoke to discover I had a wife
and three kids. It was a surprise I can tell you. Nobody
seemed to know where they had come from. I also had
a job, which was an even bigger surprise. One day I said
to the wife, "How will I ever fulfill my lifelong ambition of becoming a great outdoor photographer if I have
to work at that job all the time to support you and our
three kids?"

"Four kids," she said. "Last year it was three,
this year it's four."

I could feel Old Man Time breathing down the
back of my neck. At first I thought he was Mr. Farley,
but then I discovered it was actually our kindly old
landlord who was fond of giving me bits of advice—"Pay
da rent, fella, or else. . . ."

It was at this juncture that I decided to quit my
job and become a free-lance writer and photographer,
specializing in the Great Outdoors.

"I feel so free," I shouted, after severing rela-
tions with my employer. "No more commuting, no
more kowtowing to bosses, no more compromising my
principles!"

"No more eating!" my wife shouted. A comical
soul, she would do just about anything for a laugh, but
I thought rending her garment while pouring ashes on
her head was going a bit far.

The only things a great outdoor photographer
needs to set up in business are some film and a good
camera outfit. Film is about $1.50 a roll, and you can
pick up a good camera and accessories for not much
more than you would pay for an albino elephant that
can tap dance and sing in three languages. Since I blew
my life savings on the roll of film, I had to borrow the
money for the camera and accessories. Fortunately, I
had learned of a loan company run by about the nicest

people you could ever expect to do business with, even though they had to operate out of the back seat of a car while their new building was under construction.

After we had shaken hands on the deal, I told the loan officer, Louie, that it was none of my business but I thought they could get a better return on their money than 10 percent a year.

"A year? What year?" Louie said. He quickly explained that the interest was by the week, compounded hourly and that the only collateral was a pound of my flesh to be selected at random fifteen seconds after I missed the first payment. I exaggerate, of course. It wasn't fifteen seconds but nearly a day after I missed the first payment that my wife reported to me that two bulky hominoids had stopped by to inquire of my whereabouts. "I think they were carrying arms," she said nervously.

"You must have been mistaken," I said. "Maybe a few fingers or toes but not arms!" What kind of monsters did she think I would borrow money from, anyway?

Such was the incentive instilled in me by this visit that within a month I had the loan paid off. Editors couldn't resist my photographs.

"Terrific!" one of them said to me. "This is a fantastic shot of a woman and children in rags, a real tear-jerker. What's she got on her head, anyhow?"

"Ashes," I said, "but that's a portrait of my family and not for sale. How about this great shot of the hind foot of a bear that's just walked behind a tree?"

"I'll take it, I'll take it!" the editor said.

As time went along both my photographic skills and my reflexes improved to the point where I was shooting pictures of whole animals. I still had trouble getting good shots of leaping fish, but I produced many a fine picture wherein my catch of trout dwarfed the creel and flyrod I used for props. The fish were only eight inches long, but the creel and flyrod belonged to a dwarf.

Steadily my career progressed upward until that moment I found myself steering my car down a game trail toward an appointment with a helicopter. When I at last came ploughing out of the forest and onto the landing strip, the helicopter was still there but the pilot was nowhere to be seen. The only person around was a grizzled old packer, sitting on a log and staring at the helicopter.

"Dang things weren't meant to fly," he said to me, nodding at the chopper. "Man has to be a crazy fool to fly around these mountains in one of them eggbeaters. Give me a good mule any day."

"Don't say things like that," I told him, "because I got to go fly in that eggbeater."

"So you're the feller," he said. "Well, let's git on with it then, 'cause I'm the pilot."

The pilot's name was Lefty, and he was a pleasant but rather serious chap. "Let me explain just what we're going to do," he said, after we had climbed into the cockpit. "If you understand what's happening, you won't worry so much about us crackin' up. I always like my passengers to just relax and enjoy the ride. Hell, there's no sense in both of us being terrified."

As we lifted off and made a quick clean sweeping turn up over a wall of pine trees, I concealed my modest anxiety under an expression of disinterest and a hint of boredom.

"Nervous?" Lefty shouted at me.

"Not at all," I shouted back.

"Good," he said. "Then maybe you'll let go of my leg. You're cutting off the circulation."

Once we were on our way, the pilot reached forward and patted a little statue of St. Christopher, the patron saint of travelers, mounted on the instrument panel.

"Catholic?" I asked.

"No," he said. "Cautious."

Lefty was a good tour guide. He pointed out miniature deer far below and a herd of elk galloping along like tall ants.

"There goes a bear!" he shouted. "Look at that rascal run! Must think we're a bear hawk!"

As we pounded up over a steep, thickly forested hillside, he indicated a tiny clearing. "Last year about this time I had to put the chopper down right there."

"Gosh," I said. "That clearing doesn't look big enough to land a helicopter in."

"Shoot," he replied, "until we landed, there wasn't a clearing there at all. We mowed down trees like tall grass. Flipped plumb upside down and spun like a top. Really held our attention for a few moments. Now there you go, cuttin' off the circulation in my leg again!"

"Sorry," I said. "I just became engrossed in your story."

A sheer rock cliff that seemed a mile high loomed directly in front of us, and Lefty showed every intention of flying us smack into it.

"I got to cut out the chatter now 'cause we're coming to the scary part," he said.

"The scary part?"

"Yup, we got to catch the elevator."

"Elevator?"

He quickly explained that because of the altitude and the limited power of the helicopter, he had to put the chopper right in close to the cliff so we could ride up on the strong updraft. "St. Christopher, don't fail me now!" he said.

The elevator ride was indeed an exhilarating experience. I broke the world's record for longest sustained inhale while the pilot kept mumbling something about a valley of death. In a second we came zooming up over the top of the cliff, where Lefty cut a sporty little figure eight and set us down on the mountain peak.

He wet his finger and marked up an invisible score in the air. "St. Christopher 685, Death 0."

What, you have probably asked, could have prompted me to risk life, limb, and my meager breakfast to soar up to this barren windblown pinnacle of rock? The answer is that I was there to photograph a mountain-goat-trapping expedition. The Idaho Fish and Game department was capturing goats, ferrying them off the mountain via helicopter, and transplanting them in a goatless area of the state. The action went like this: a goat would be lured into a net trap, then two Fish and Game men would jump on him, wrestle him to the ground, and give him a shot of tranquilizer to calm him down. The goat, for his part, would try to tap dance on the heads of his molesters while simultaneously trying to spindle them on his horns. There would be this ball of furious activity, consisting of legs, arms, eyes, hooves, horns, bleats, bellows, grunts and curses, until one of the F and G men would shout, "Quick, the tranquilizer!"

A hypodermic needle would flash amid the tangle of goat and men. "Got it! How's that?"

"Great," the other man would say. "Now let's see if you can get the next one in the goat."

It was all very amusing and provided me with some fine action shots. The one problem, as I saw it, was that the trappers tended to favor the smaller goats.

What I wanted was some photos of them tangling with a really big billy, right up on the edge of the cliff where it would be exciting, but they chose to ignore my suggestions, claiming that the small goats more than satisfied their thirst for excitement.

At last I persuaded Jack McNeel, a tall, lean conservation officer, to have a go at one of the big goats. I situated myself on an outcropping of rock close to the net at the edge of the cliff, camera at the ready. Presently, the King Kong of mountain goats came sauntering up the hill and strolled into the trap for a lick of the salt block used for bait. When the trap closed on him, that goat went absolutely bananas. Rock, hair, and pieces of goat trap flew in all directions. As Jack and another F and G man came racing toward the raging animal, I knew I was about to get the greatest action shots in the history of outdoor photography. But just as Jack was about to close in, the goat got a horn under the bottom edge of the trap and sent the contraption flying ten feet in the air. Caught up in the excitement of the chase and without thinking, McNeel made a lunge and grabbed the billy by a horn. What happened next was more than I had ever even dreamed of in my career as a wildlife photographer. I was absolutely awestruck by the sheer power of the spectacle. Perhaps you've never seen a mountain goat twirl a six-foot-four man over his head like a baton, but if you ever get the chance it's well worth the price of admission. That nifty little performance, however, was just the warm up for the grand finale. The grand finale was where the goat made a great running leap out over the edge of the cliff, Jack still clinging desperately to his horn.

I have not the slightest doubt that the conservation officer saved that goat's life, not to mention his own. As he hurtled out into space, McNeel reached down and grabbed a branch of a stunted little tree growing on the edge of the cliff. For an instant they dangled there, Jack clinging to the branch with one hand and to the goat with the other. Then he dropped the billy, who landed on an inch-wide ledge twenty feet below and galloped off. It was all absolutely stunning.

Jack crawled back up over the edge of the cliff and lay on the rock, panting. "I guess that must have made some picture, hunh?" he said.

"Picture?" I said. "What picture?" For the first time since the action started, I stared down at the camera clenched in my sweating hands.

I HAD FORGOTTEN TO TAKE THE PICTURE!

Like the great fish that got away and the great trophy buck that was missed, the great outdoor photograph that wasn't taken leaves no proof of its existence. But Jack McNeel of the Idaho Fish and Game department will swear to the absolute truth of what I have reported here. At least the last time I saw him, he was still swearing about it.

My spirit had been broken, and then and there on that windswept mile-high slab of granite I gave up my career as a great outdoor photographer. I packed my gear, shuffled up to the peak, and climbed aboard the waiting helicopter.

"Now comes the bad part," the pilot said. "Just sit back and relax."